Gustav Klimt:
130 Paintings in Close Up

By Matt Johnson

First Edition

*****

Gustav Klimt: 130 Paintings in Close Up
*****

Foreword

Gustav Klimt was an Austrian symbolist painter, whose primary subject was the female body. His paintings, murals, and sketches are marked by a sensual eroticism, which is especially apparent in his pencil drawings. He was Vienna's most famous advocator of Art Nouveau, or, as the style was identified in Germany, "youth style". He is remembered as one of the famous decorative artists of the 20 century, and he also created one of the century's most important examples of erotic art. Primarily flourishing as a conservative academic painter, his run into with more modern trends in European art encouraged him to build up his own free and frequently out of this world style. His place as the co-founder and first president of the Vienna Secession also ensured that this style would become broadly prominent - though Klimt's direct authority on other artists was partial.

Klimt attended the Vienna University of Arts and Crafts in 1876, and formed the "Company of Artists" with his two brothers and a friend, after which he was awarded the Golden Order of Merit from the Emperor of Vienna. In 1892, his father and one of his brothers died, leaving him responsible for their families. The family tragedy also affected his artistic vision, which helped him develop his own personal style.

Throughout his life, although he was a controversial painter due to his subject matter, he was made an honorary member of the Universities of Vienna and of Munich. He was also a founding member and president of the Vienna Secession, which sought to create a platform for new and unconventional artists, bring new artists to Vienna, and created a magazine to showcase its member' work.

Klimt lived a simple, cloistered life, in which he avoided other artists and café society. He often wore a long robe, sandals, and no undergarments. He also had many discreet affairs with women, and fathered at least 14 children. This may be an indication of his passion for women, their form and sexuality, which was the main focus of many of his works. The majority of his paintings were characterized by golden or swirling designs, spirals, and phallic shapes, depicting dominant women in erotic positions.

Klimt died in the influenza epidemic of 1918, leaving behind a posthumous legacy that few artists can rival. His paintings have brought in the highest amounts ever paid at auction.

While some critics and historians contend that Klimt's work should not be incorporated in the canon of modern art, his work - particularly his paintings after 1900 - remains striking for its visual combinations of the old and the modern, the real and the abstract. Klimt shaped his greatest work during a time of change and radical ideas, and these traits are clearly marked in his paintings.

Paintings

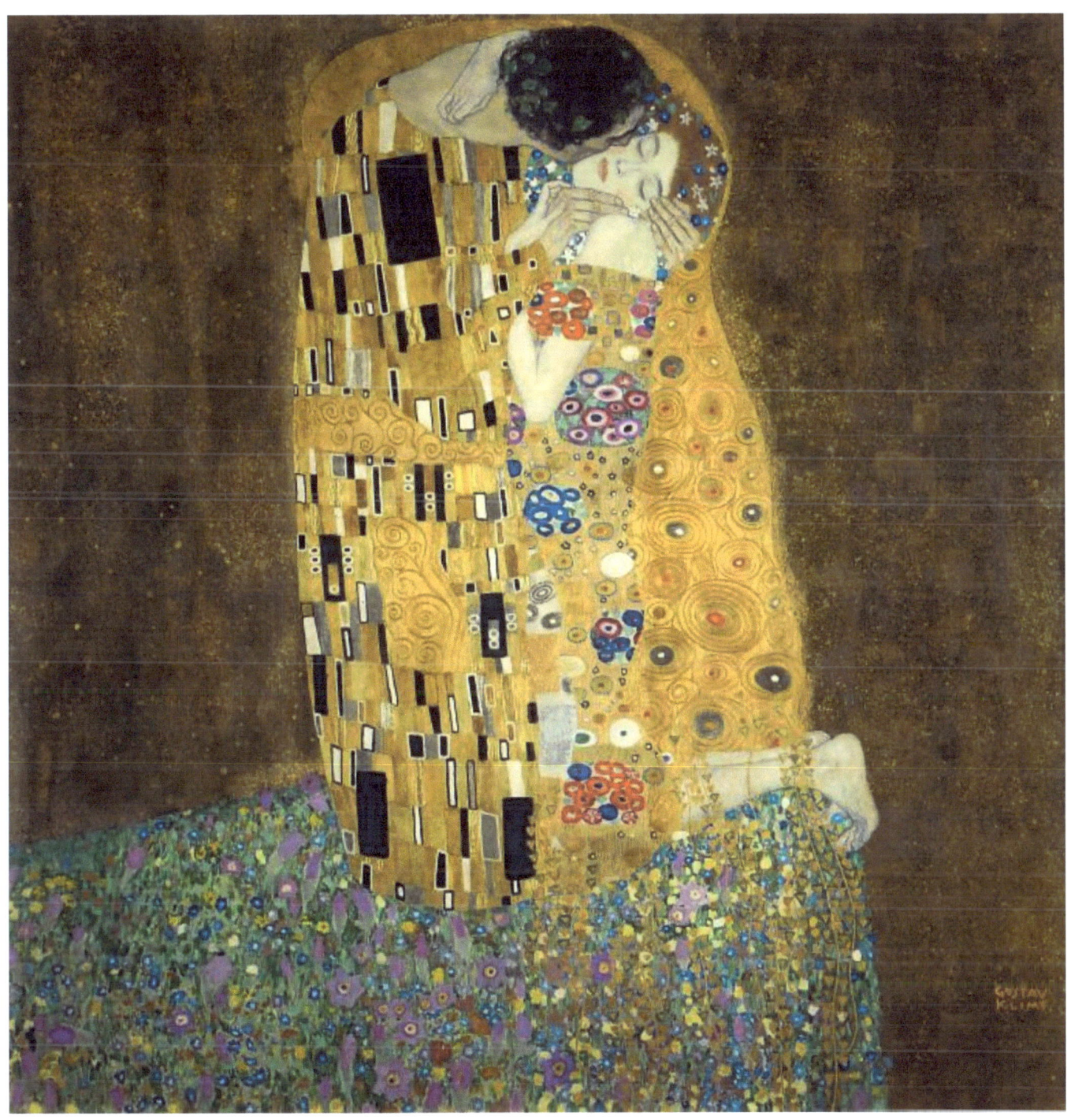

The Kiss
1907-1908, oil on canvas

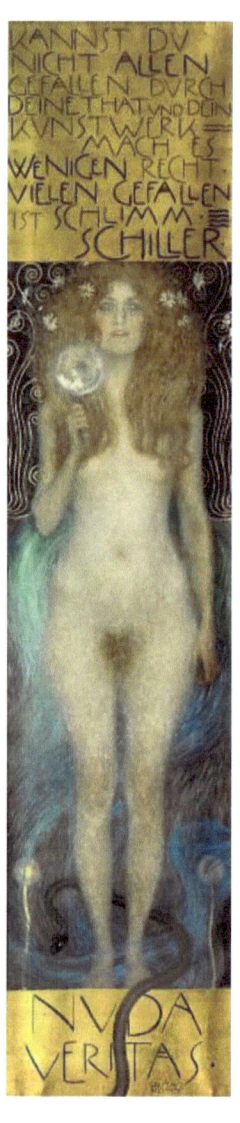

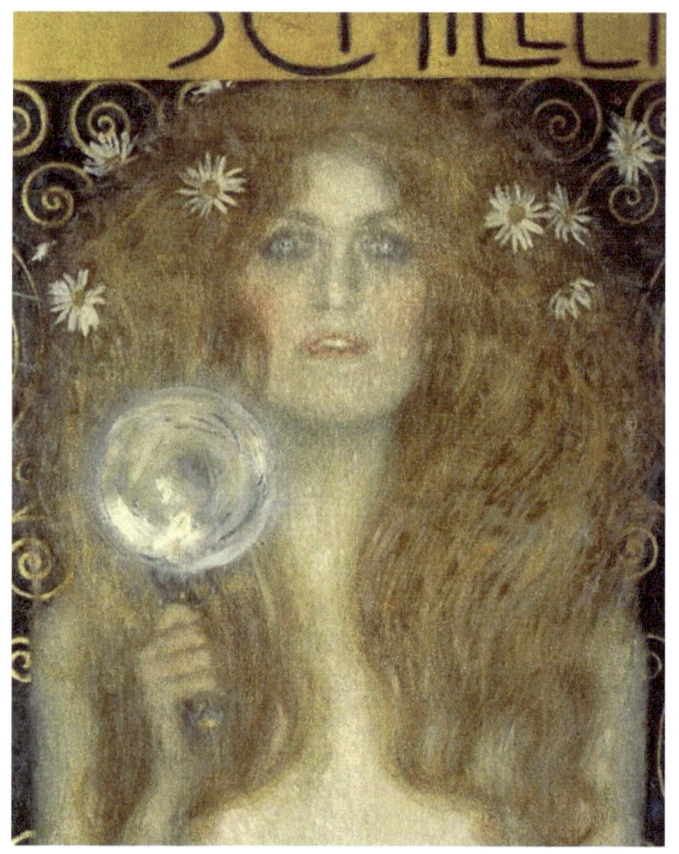

Detail

Nuda Veritas (Naked Truth)
1899, 252x56, Austrian National Library,
Wien

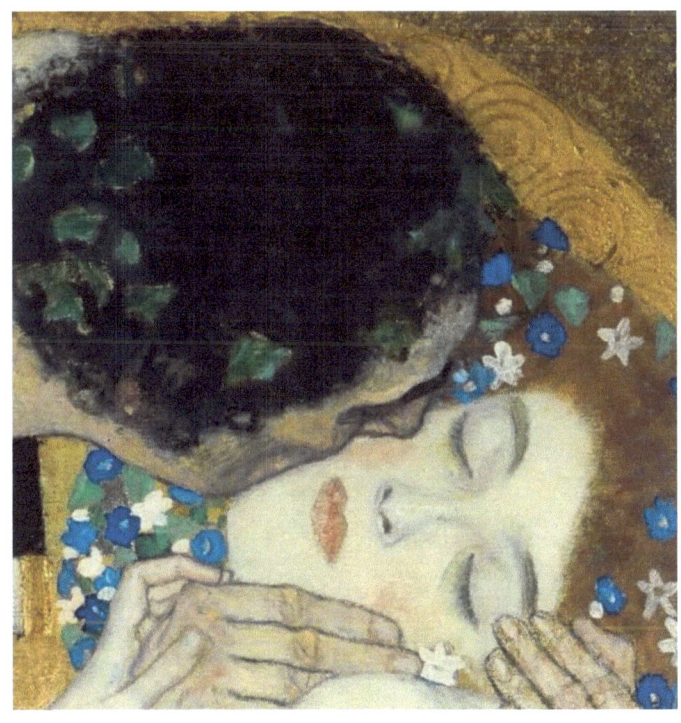

Detail

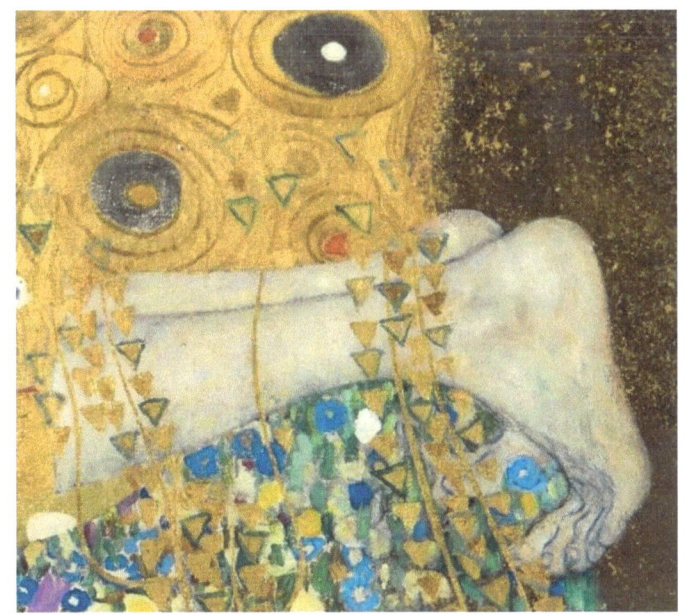

Detail

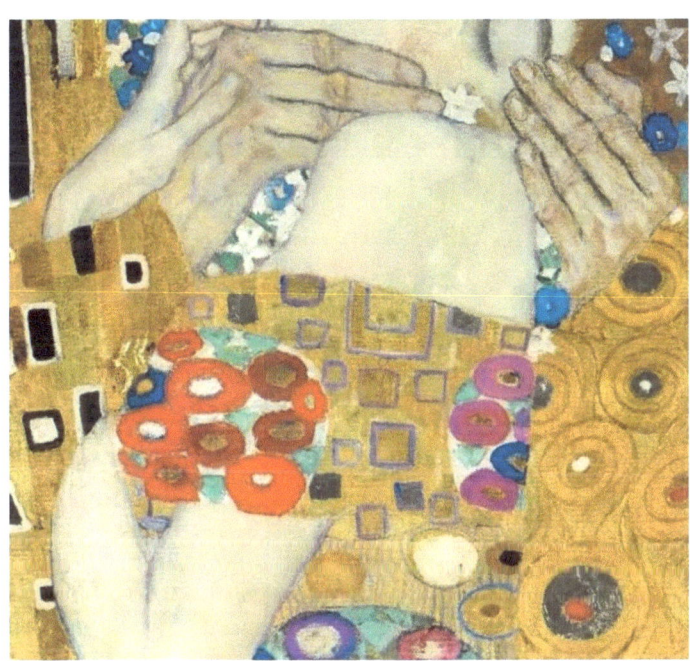

Detail

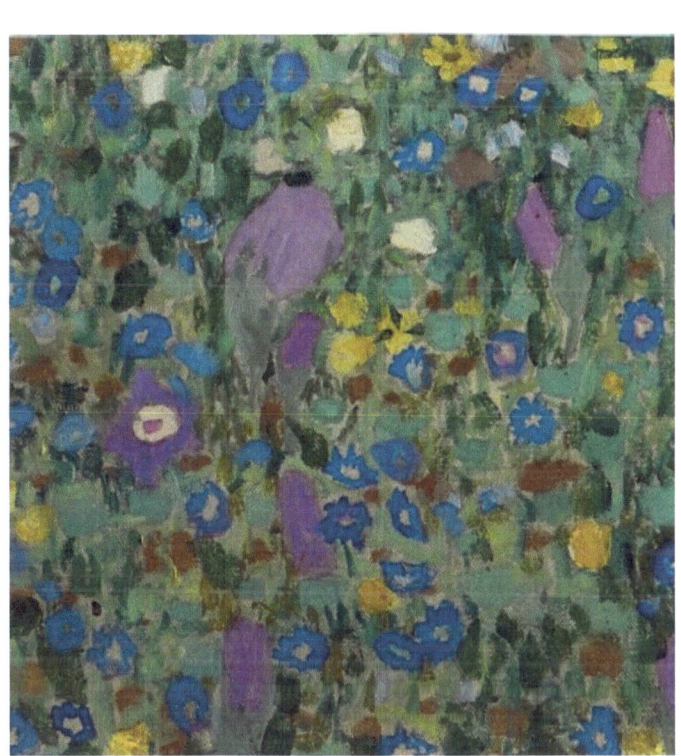

Detail

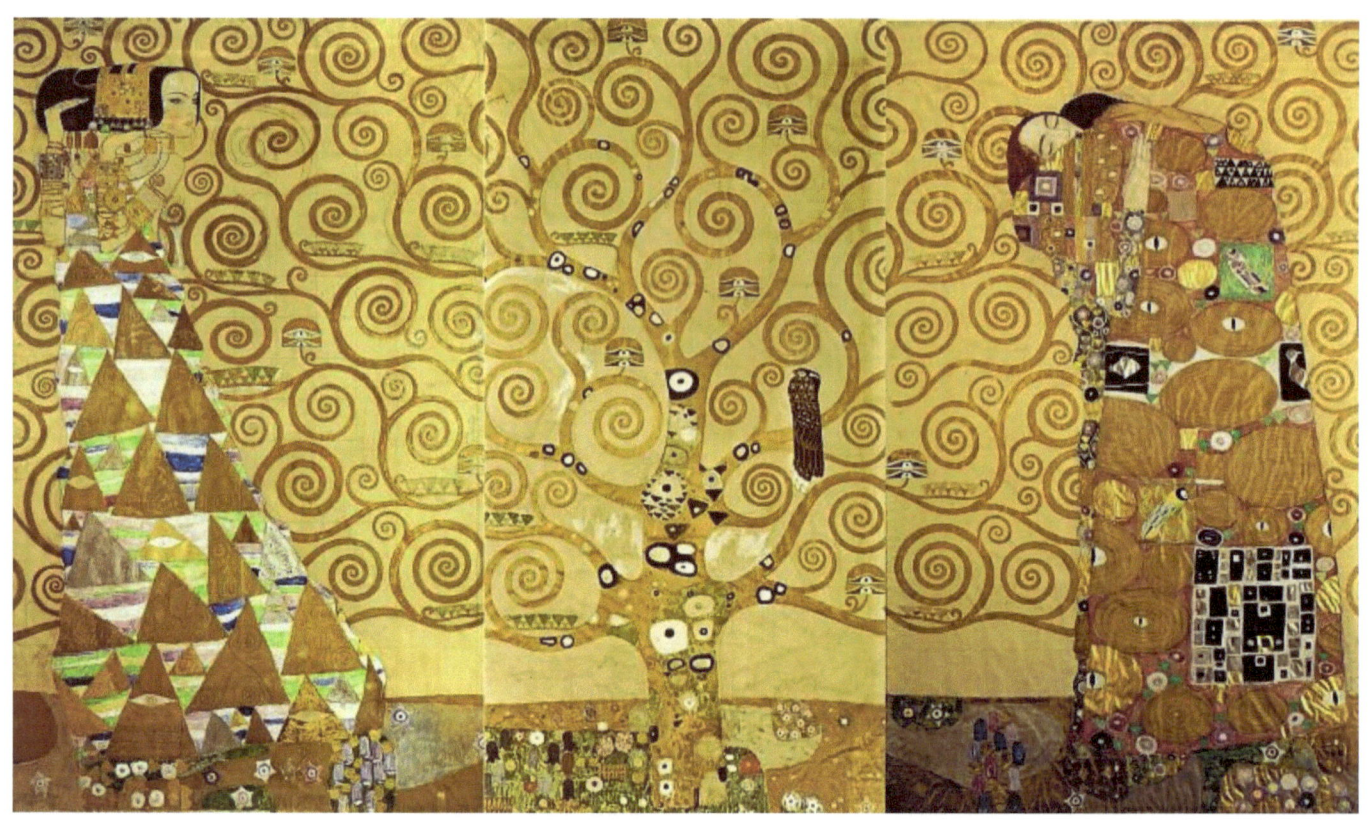

Frieze of the Villa Stoclet in Brussels
1909, oil on canvas

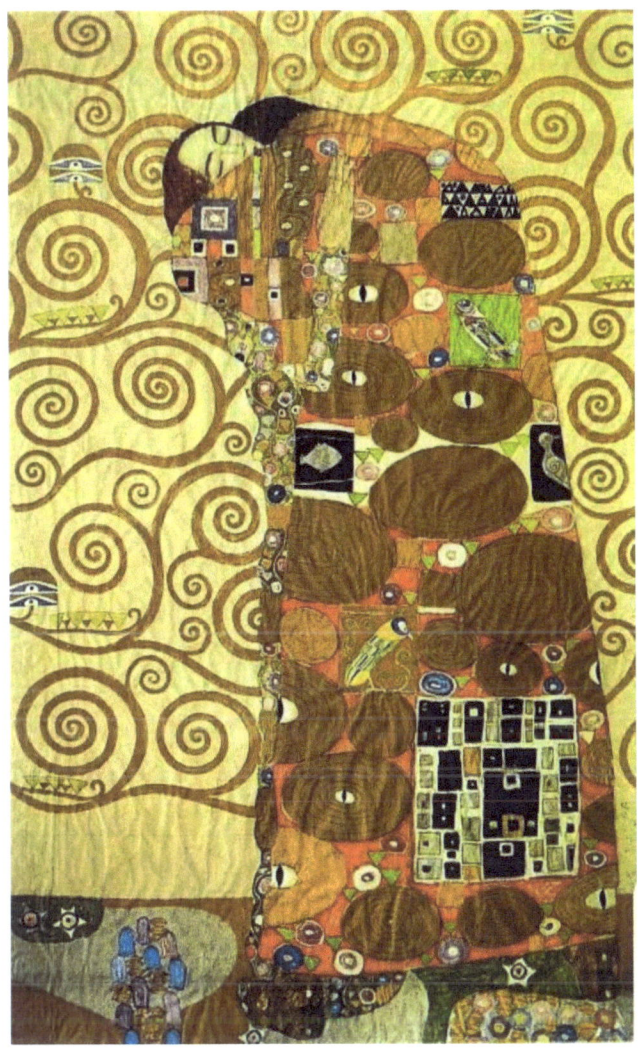

Fragment of Frieze of the Villa Stoclet in
Brussels: Fulfillment

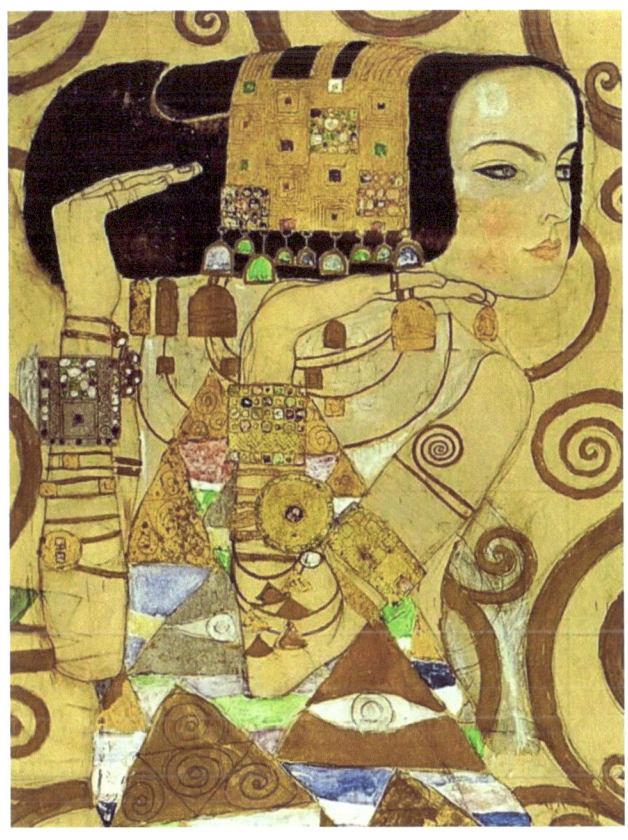

Fragment of Frieze of the Villa Stoclet in
Brussels: Expectation

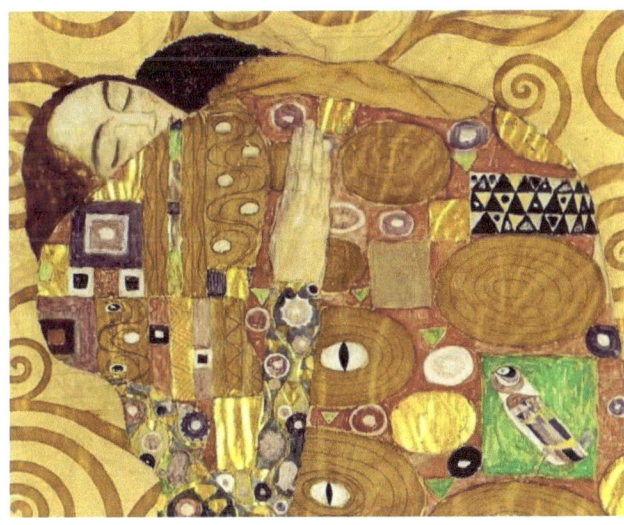

Detail

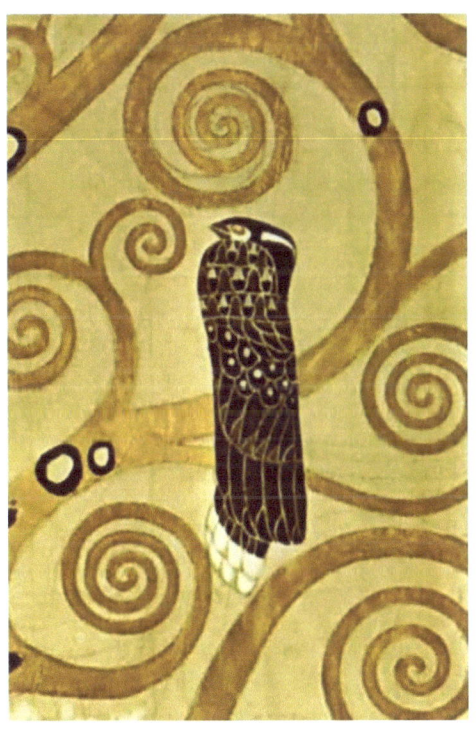

Detail

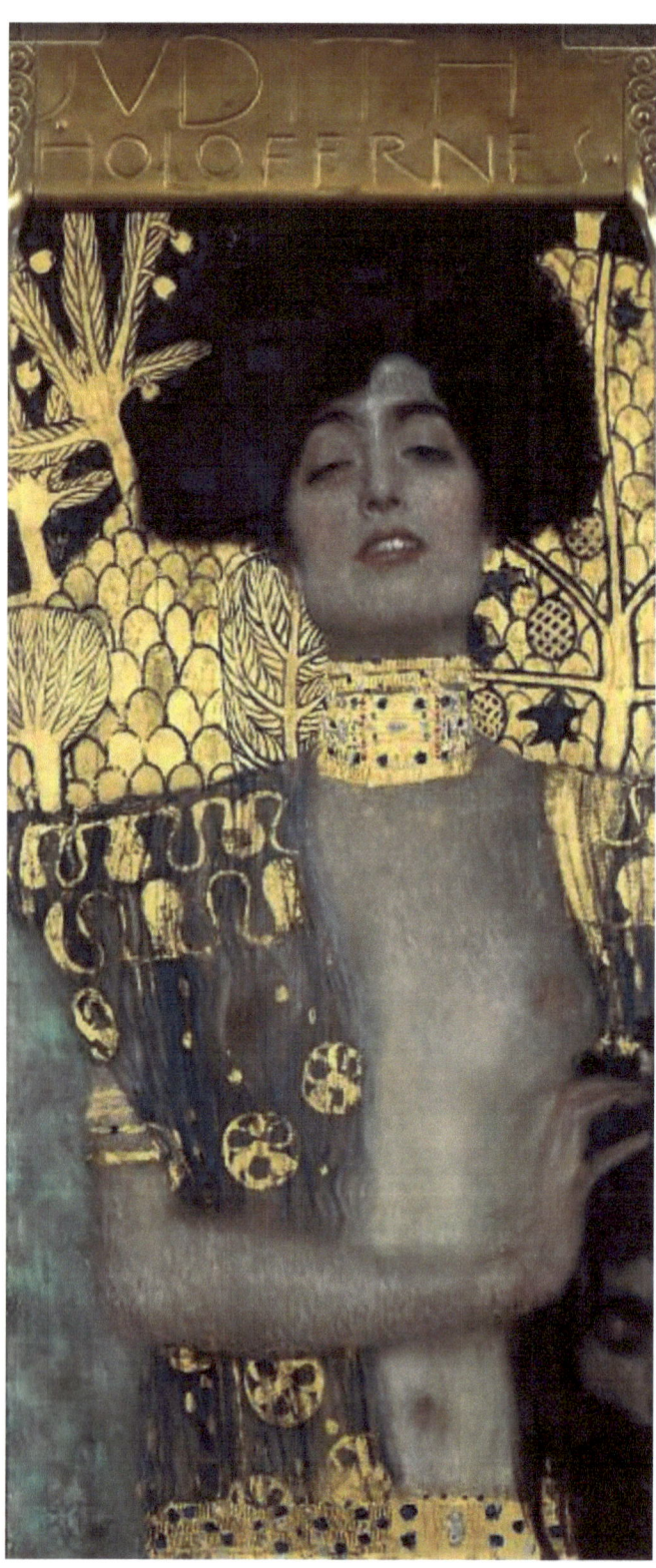

Judith and Holopherne
1901, oil on canvas

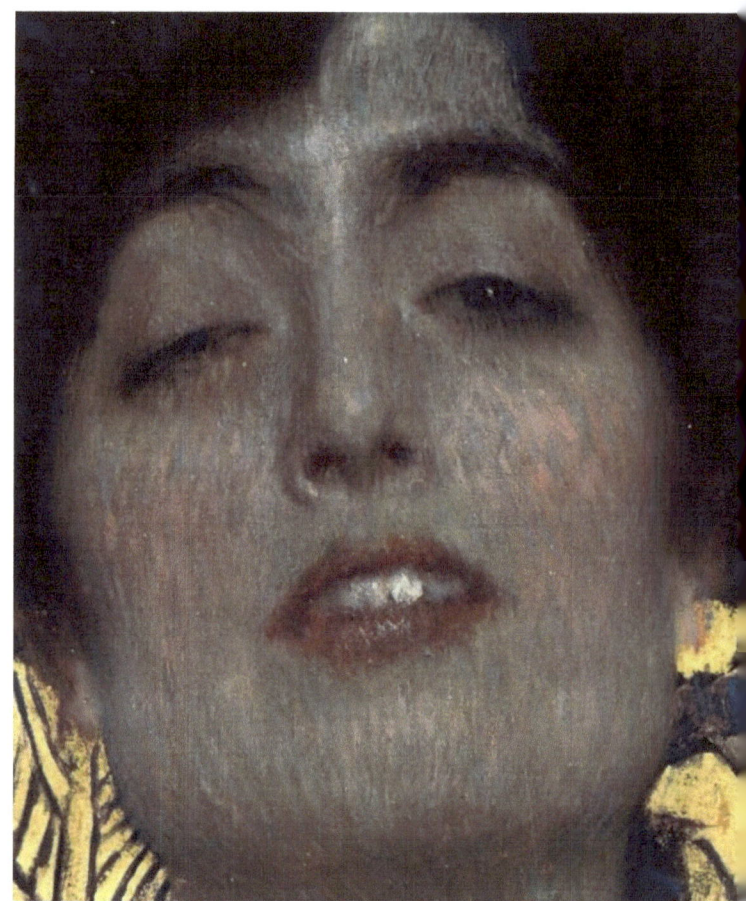

Detail

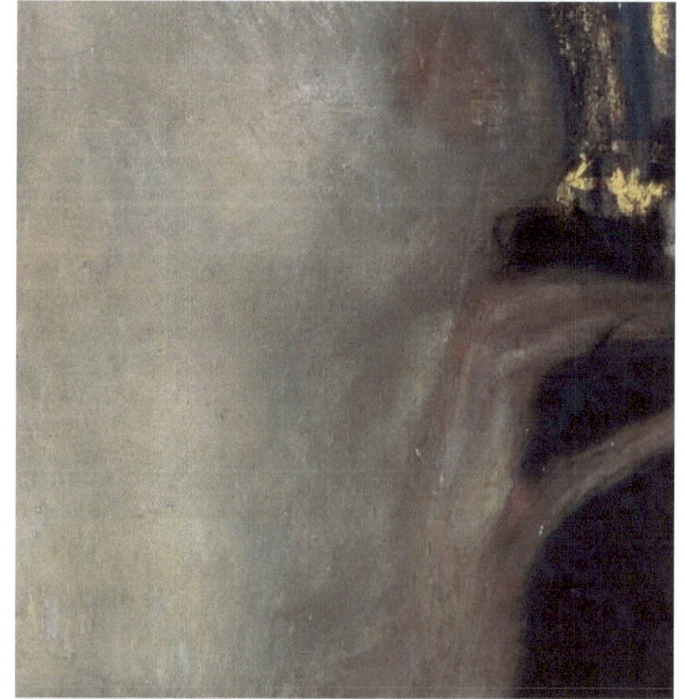

Detail

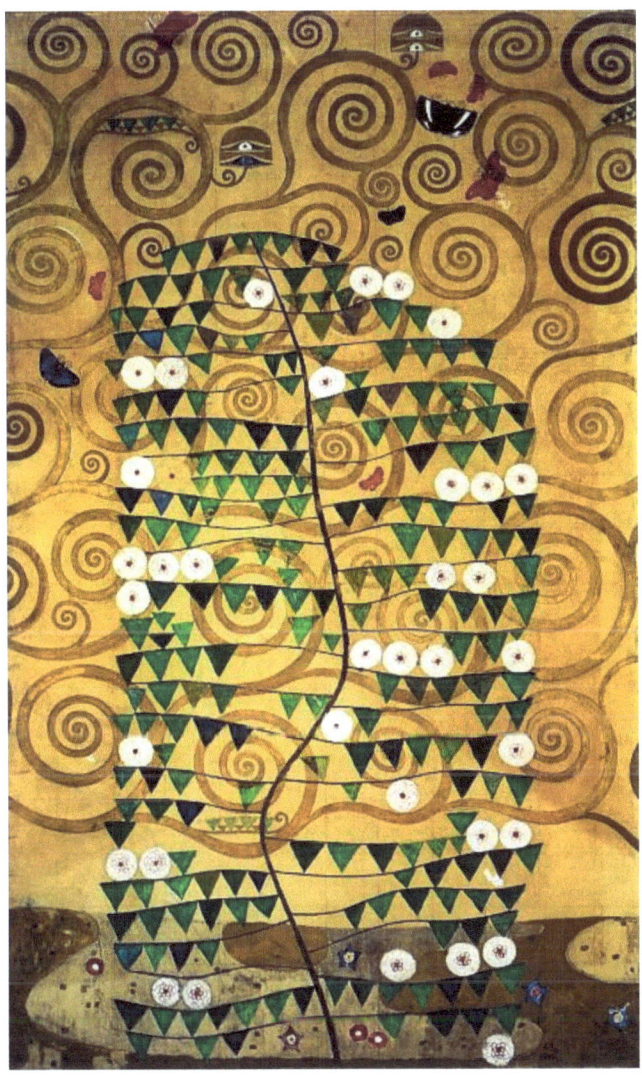

Cartoon for the frieze of the Villa Stoclet in
Brussels: right part of the tree of life
1909, oil on canvas

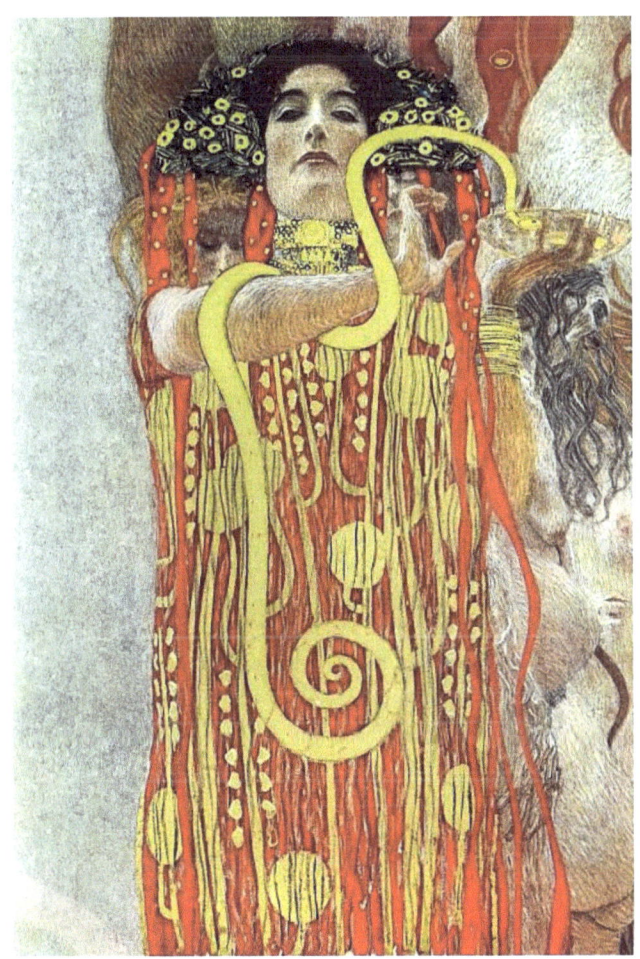

University of Vienna Ceiling Paintings
(Medicine), detail showing Hygieia
1907, oil on canvas

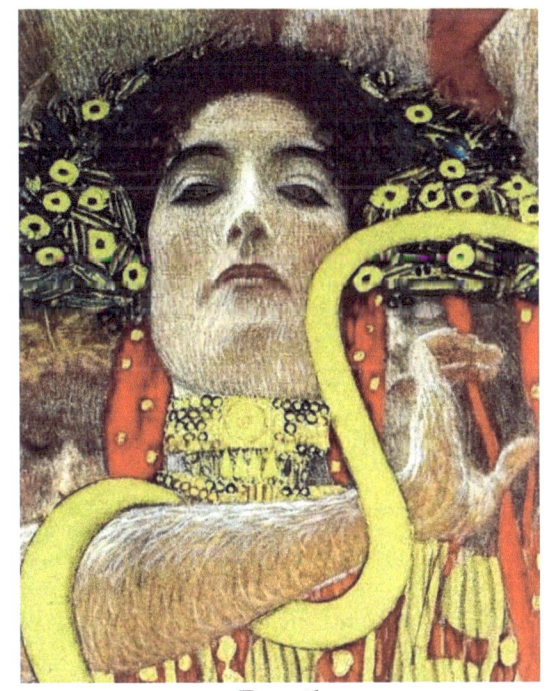

Detail

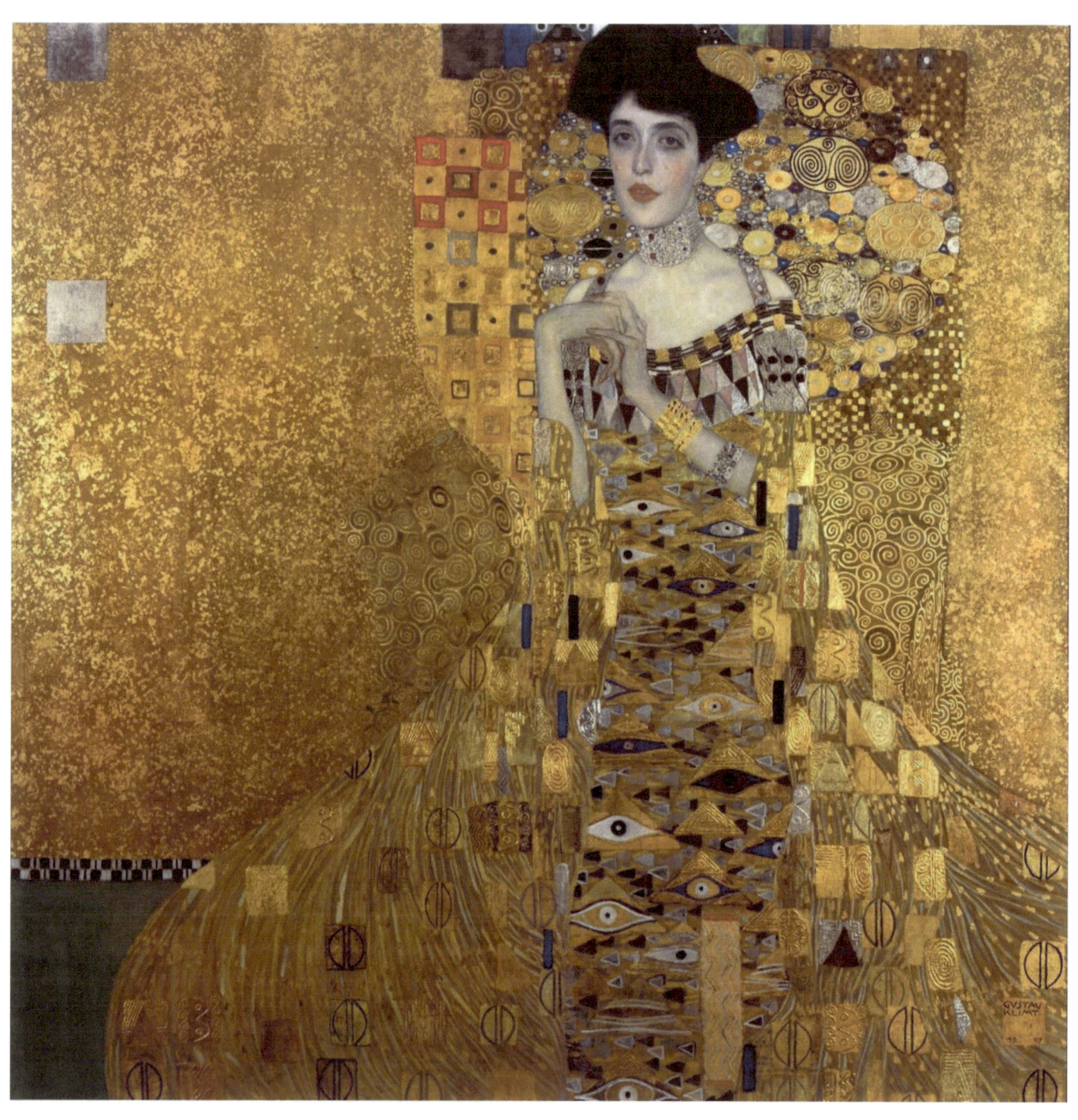

Portrait of Adele Bloch-Bauer I
1907, oil on canvas

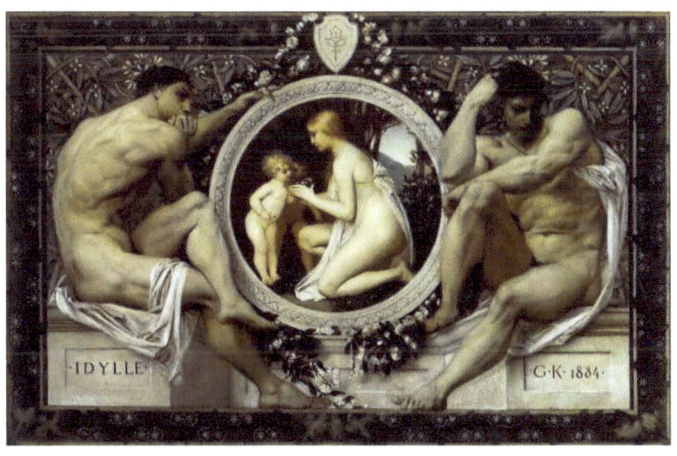

Idylle (Idylls)
1884, oil on canvas

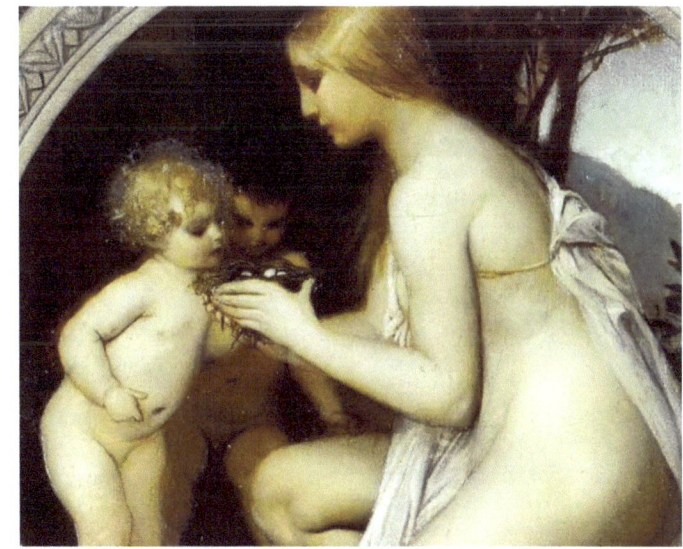

Detail

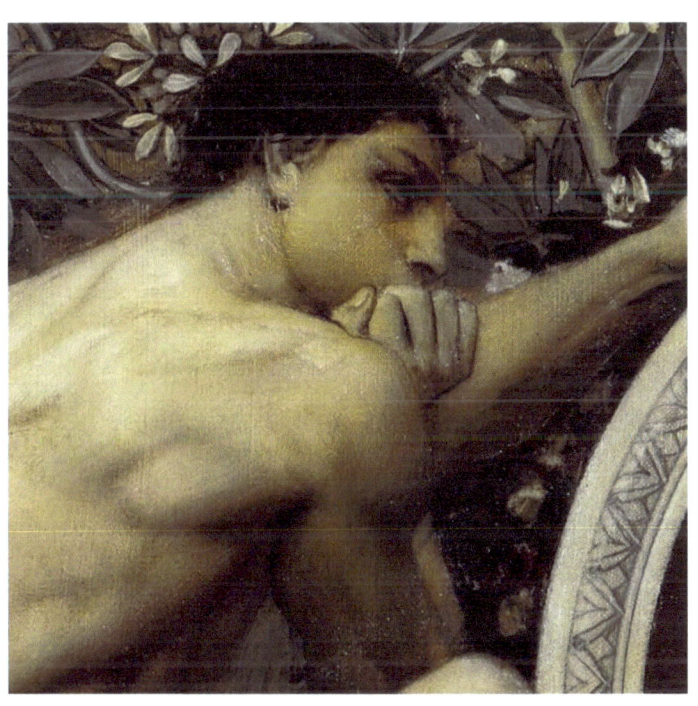

Detail

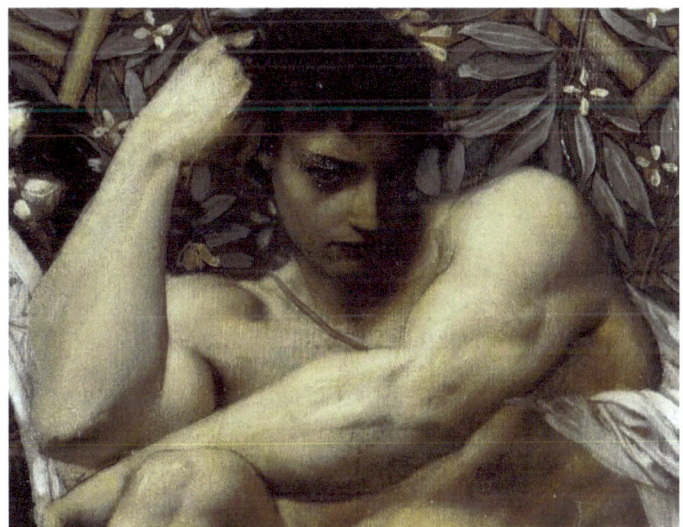

Detail

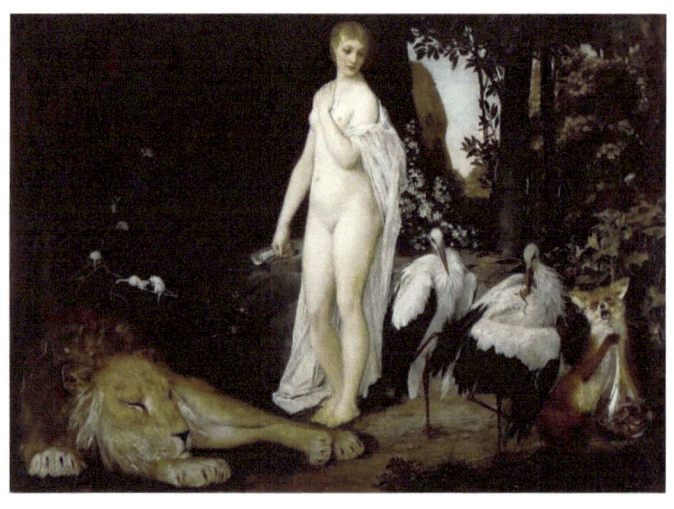

Fable
1883, oil on canvas

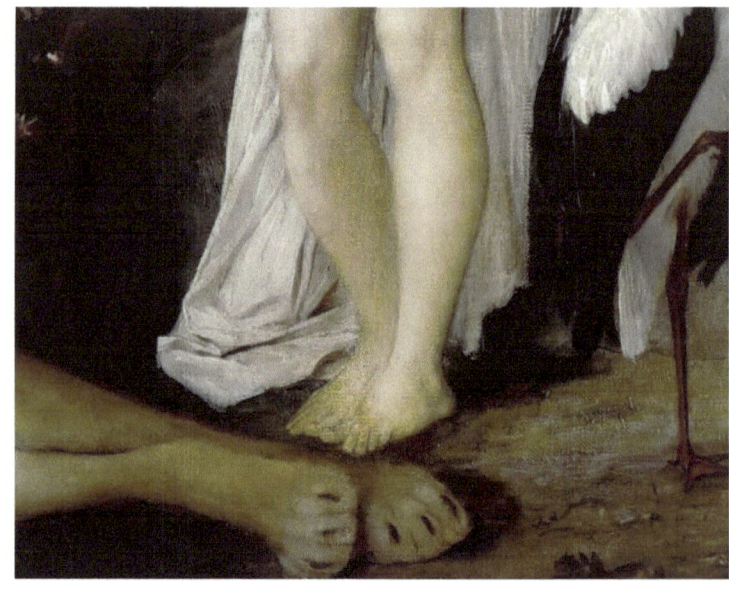

Detail

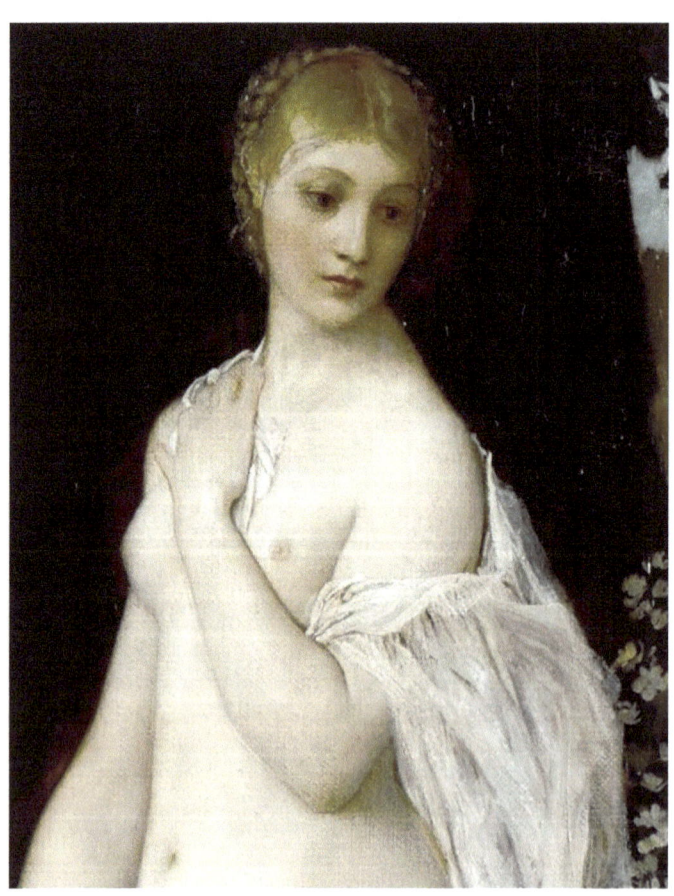

Detail

14

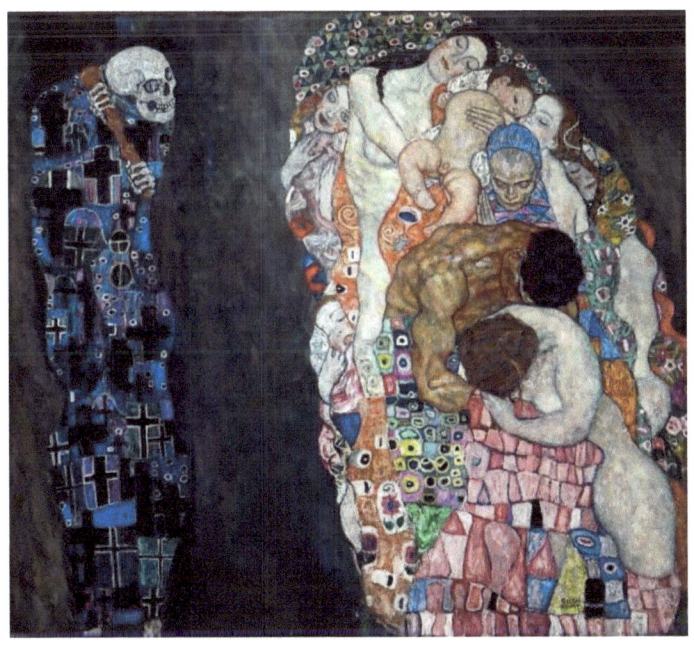

Death and Life
Painted before 1911 and revised 1915, Oil on canvas

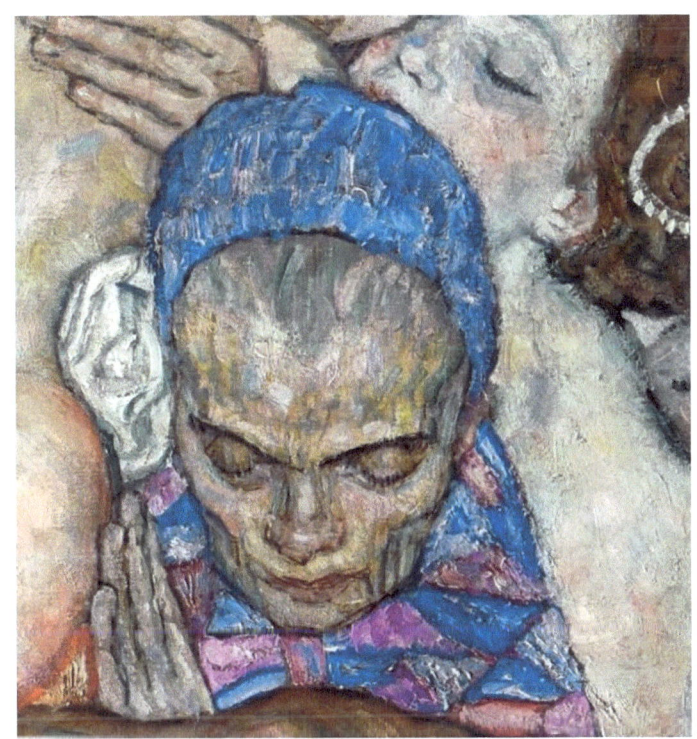

Detail

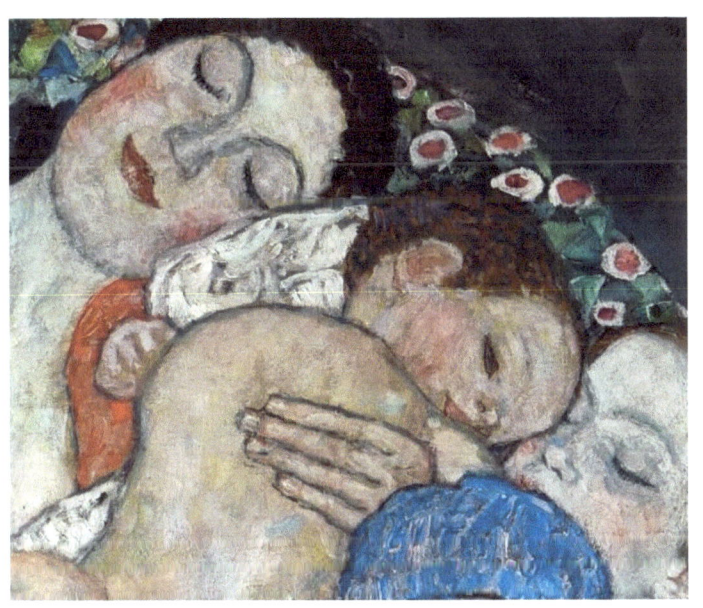

Detail

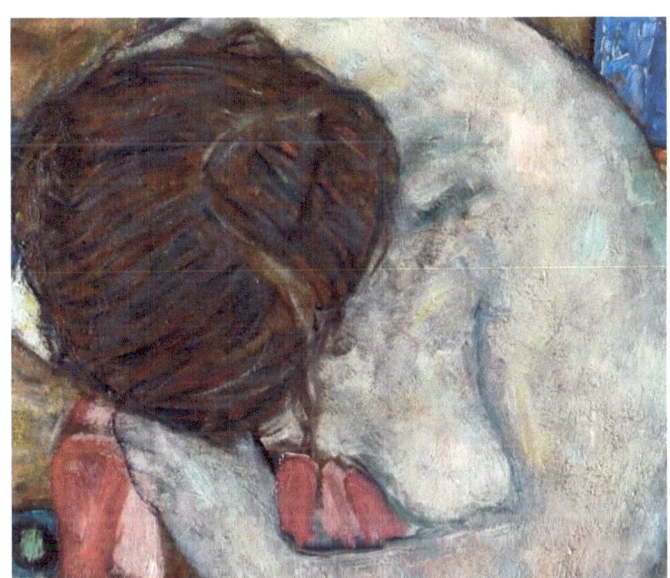

Detail

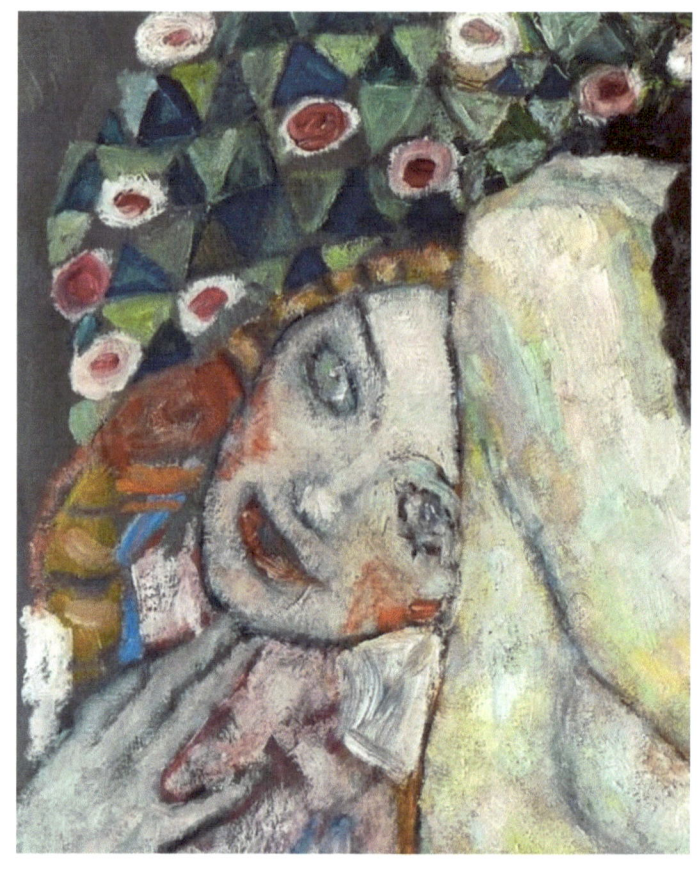

Detail

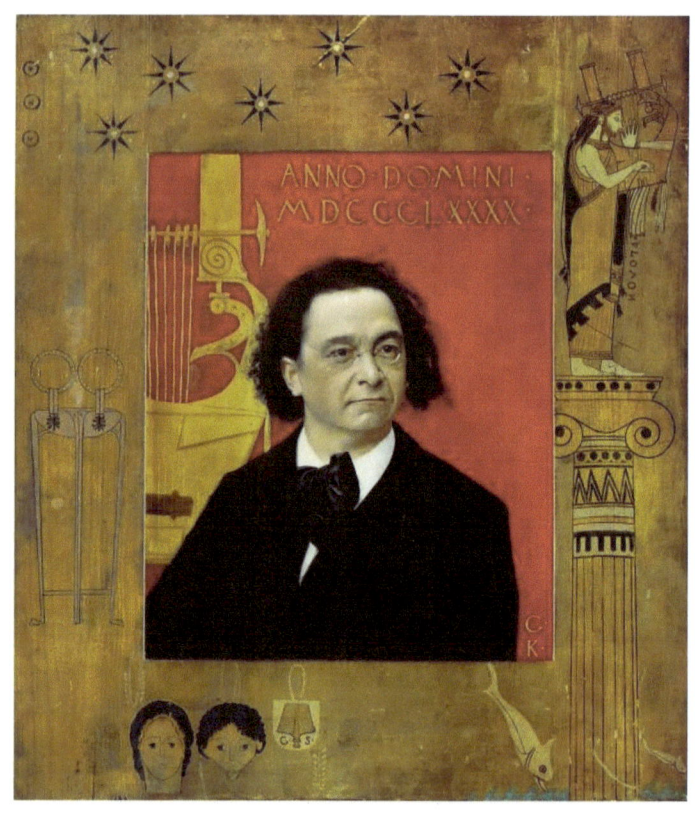

Portrait of Joseph Pembauer
1890, oil on canvas

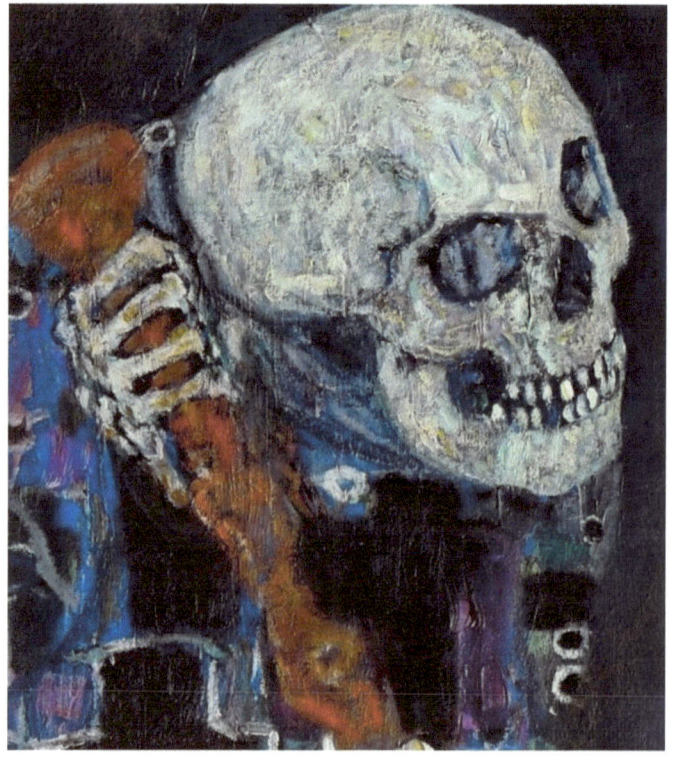

Detail

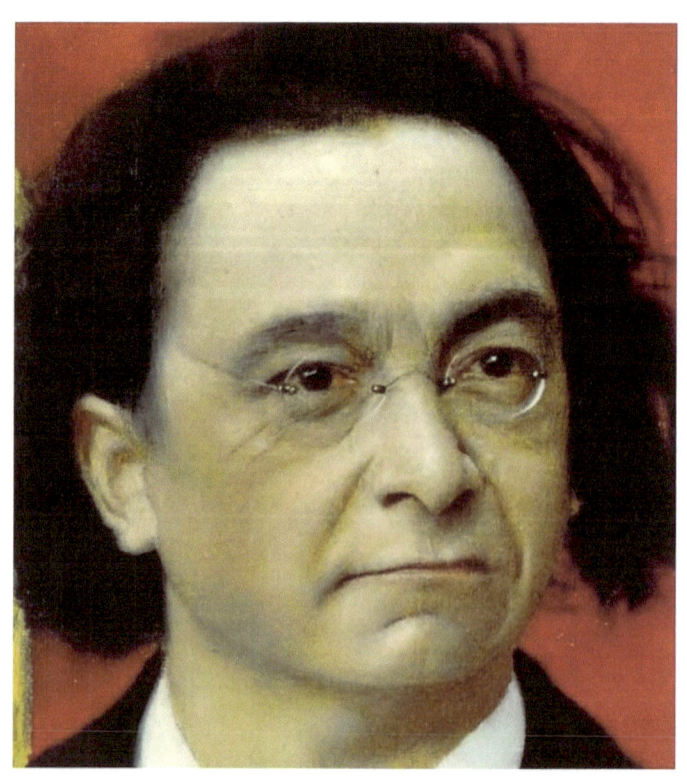

Detail

16

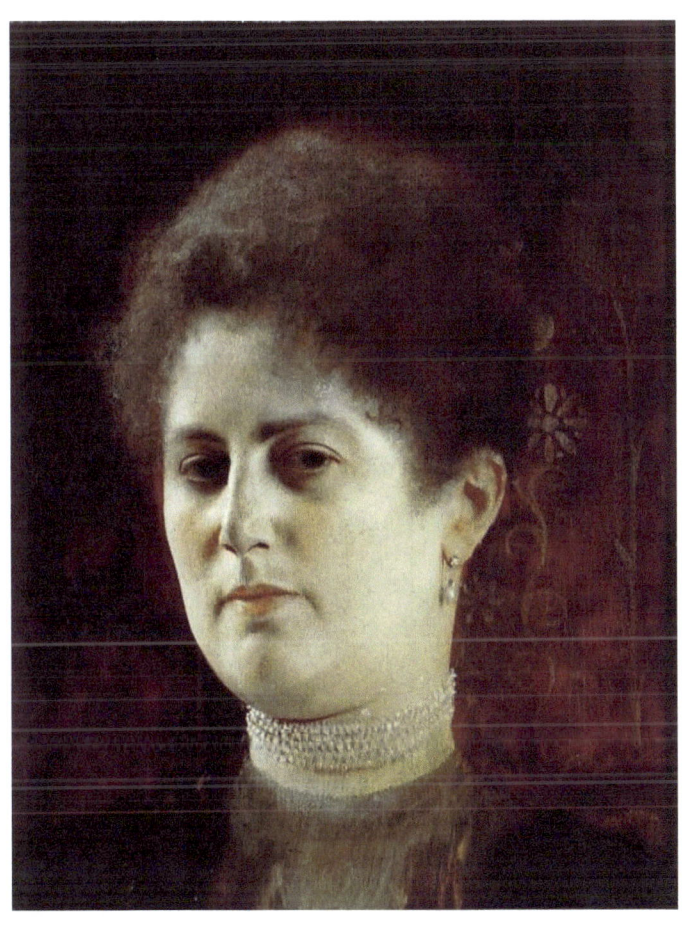

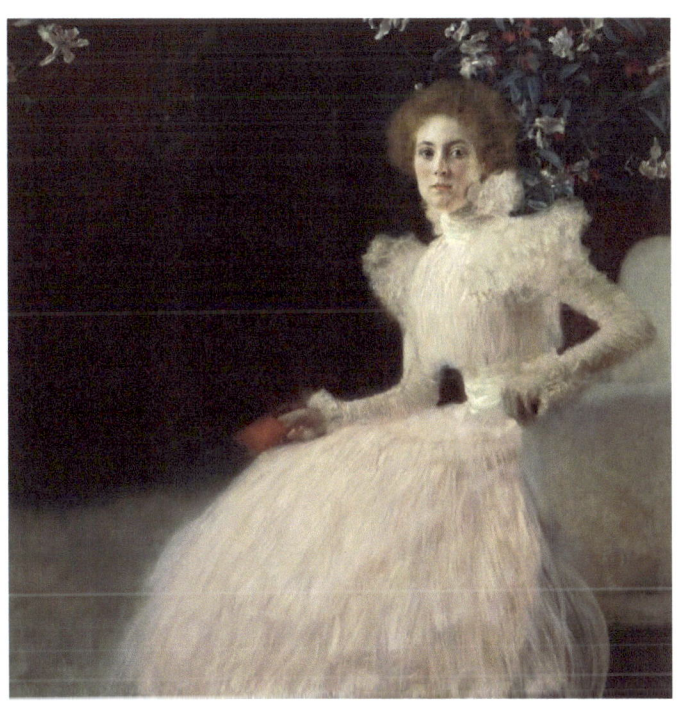

Sonja Knips
1898, oil on canvas

Portrait of a lady
1894, oil on canvas

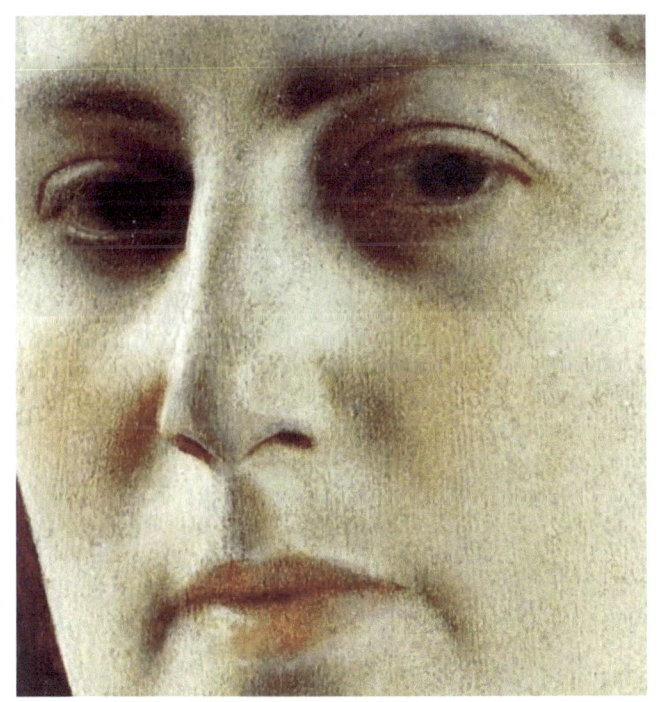

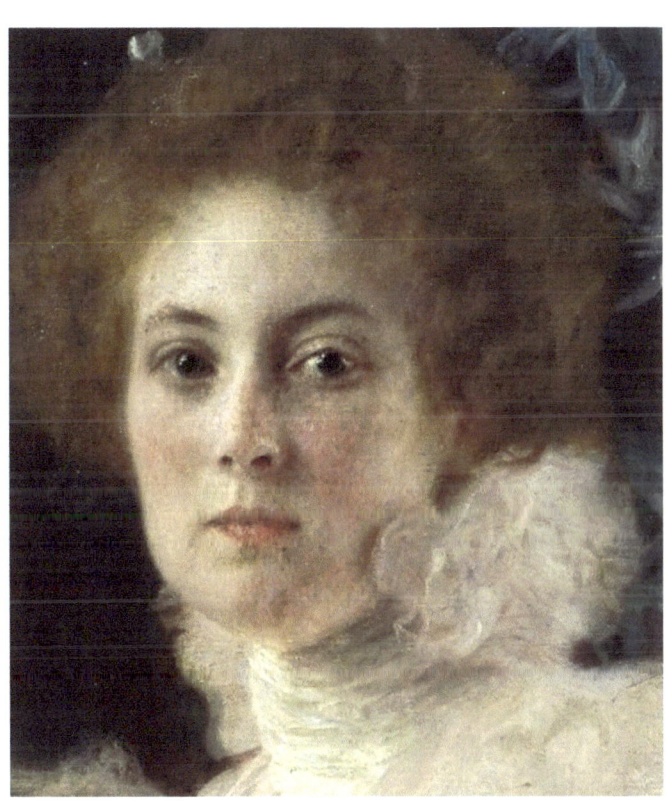

Detail

Detail

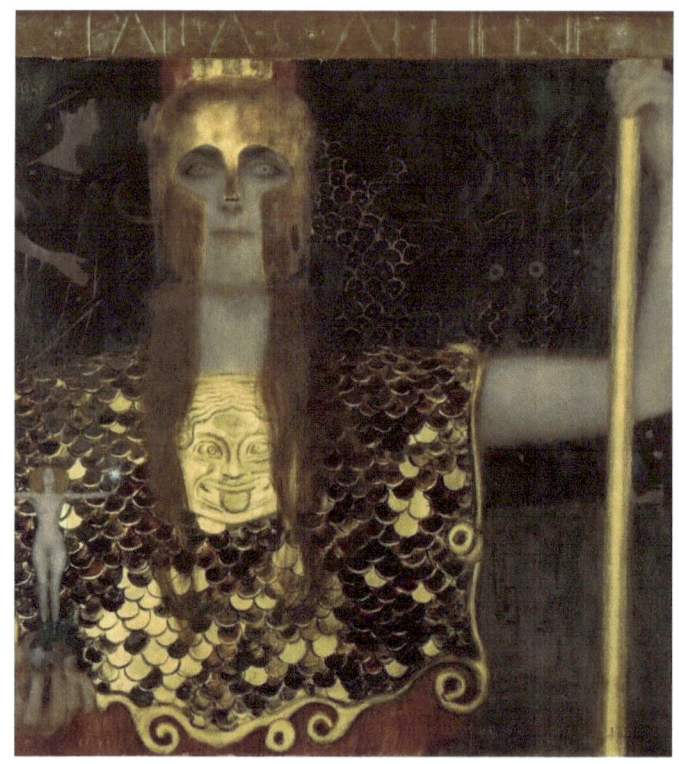

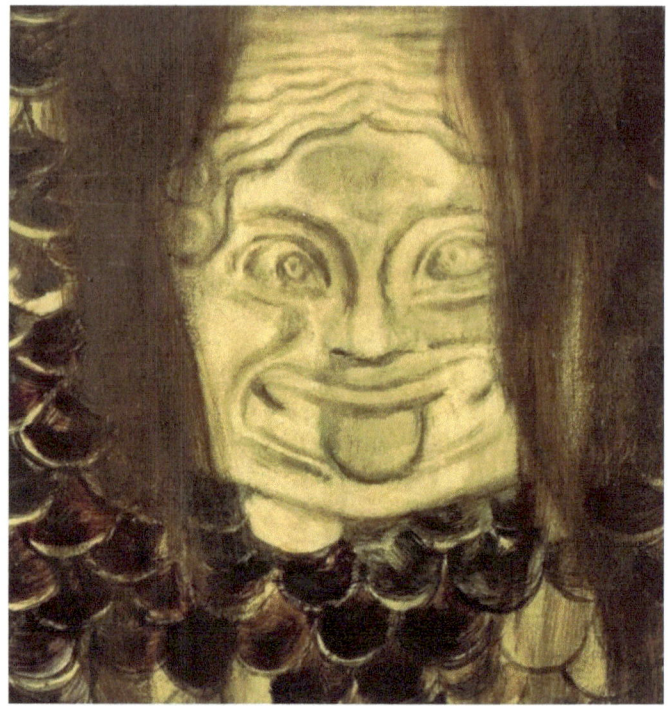

Detail

Minerva or Pallas Athena
1898, oil on canvas

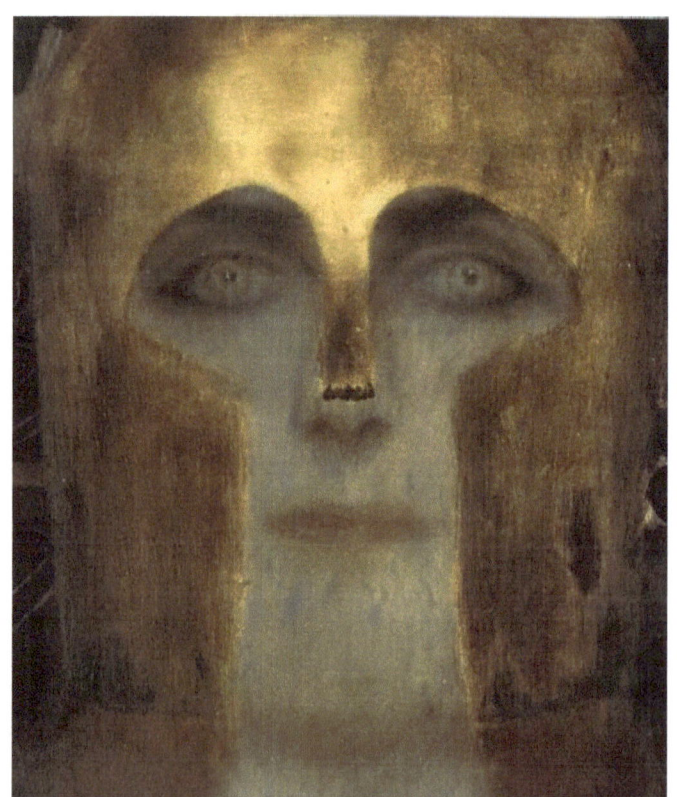

Detail

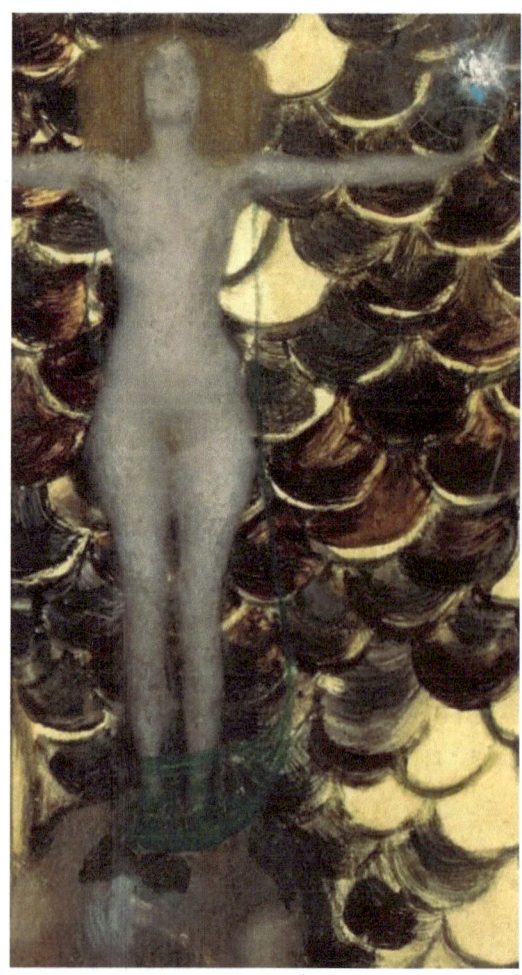

Detail

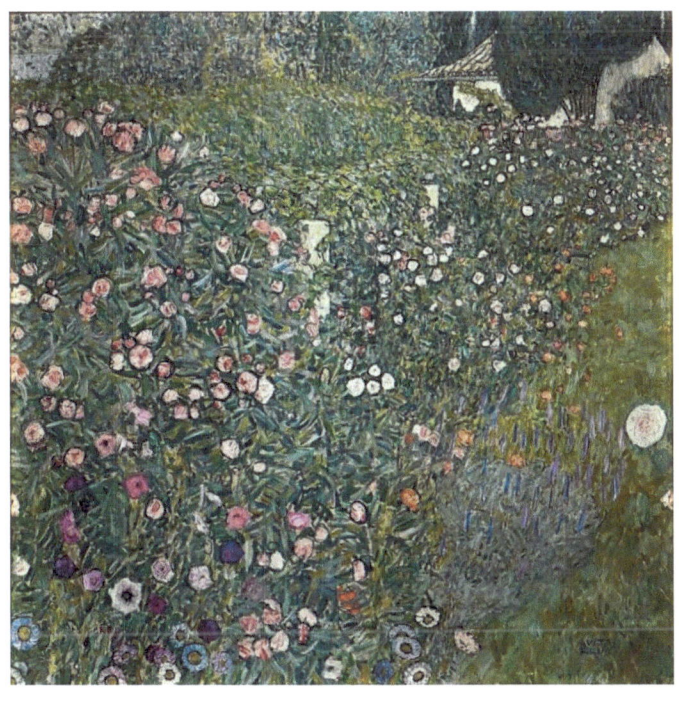

Italian Garden Landscape
Oil on canvas

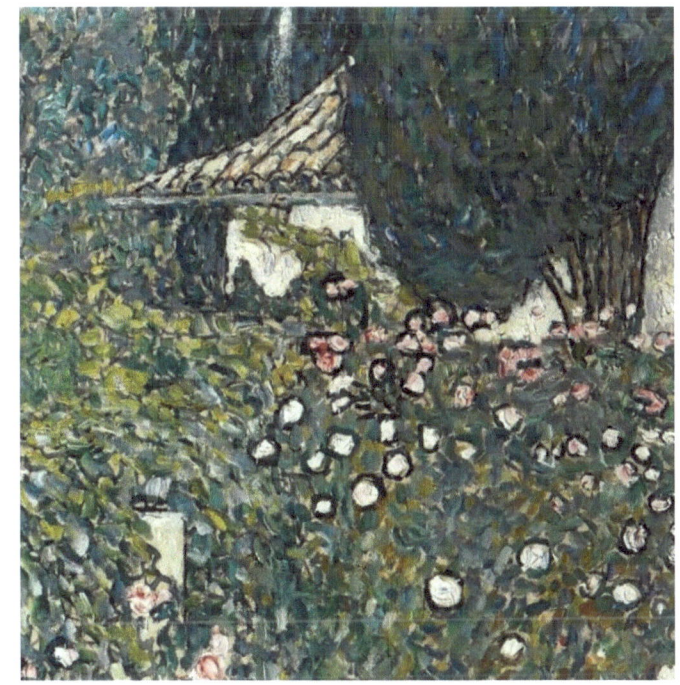

Detail

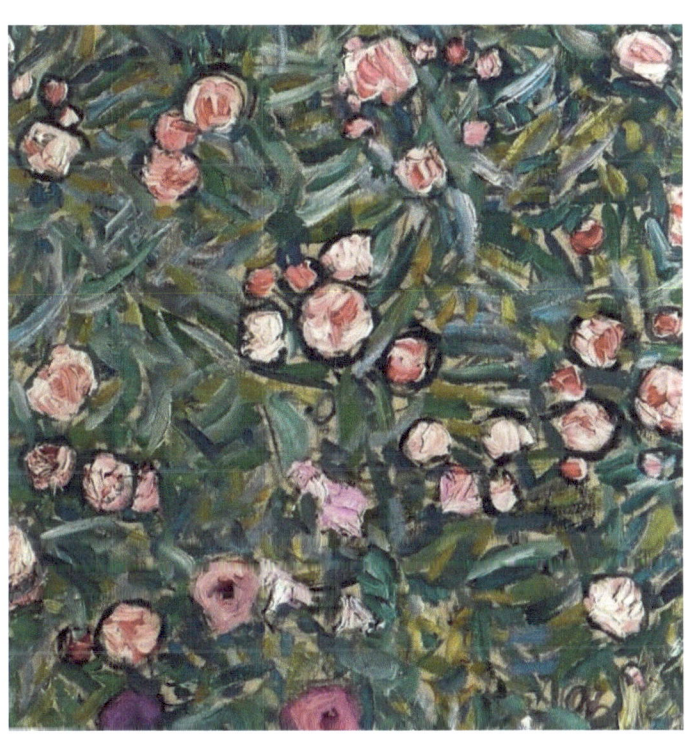

Detail

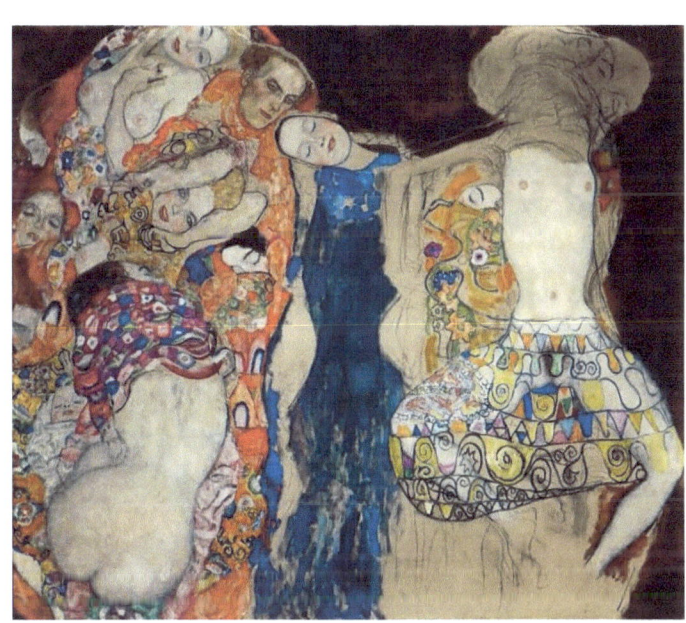

The Bride
1818, Oil on canvas

19

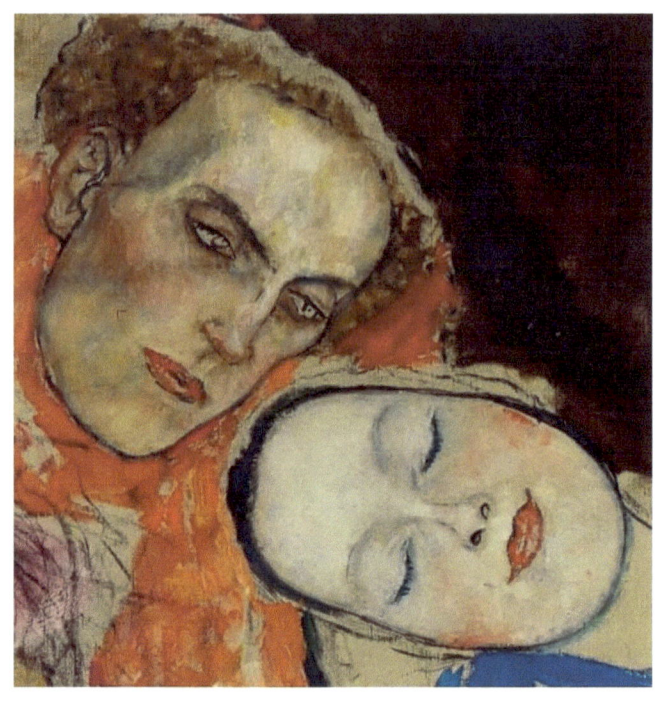

Detail

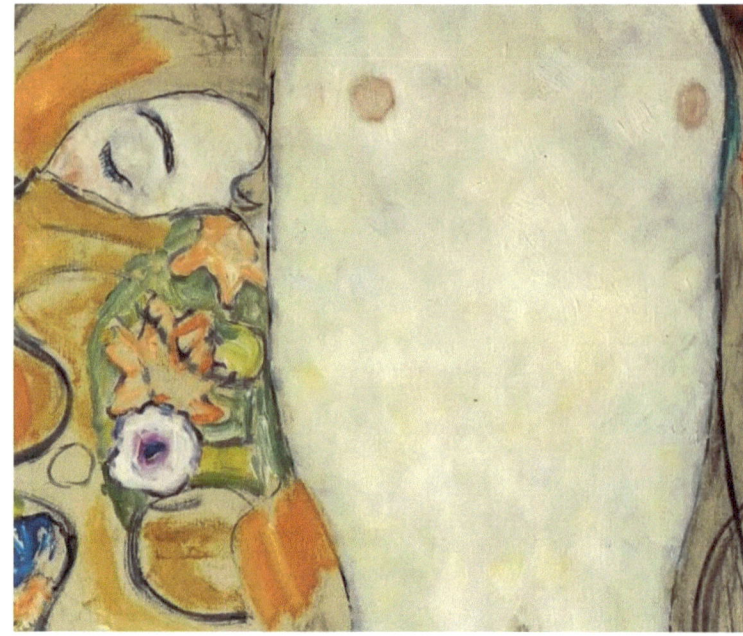

Detail

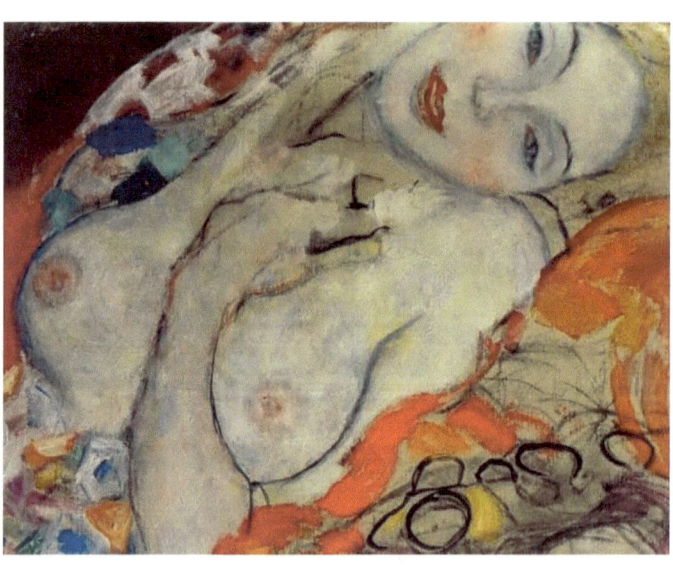

Detail

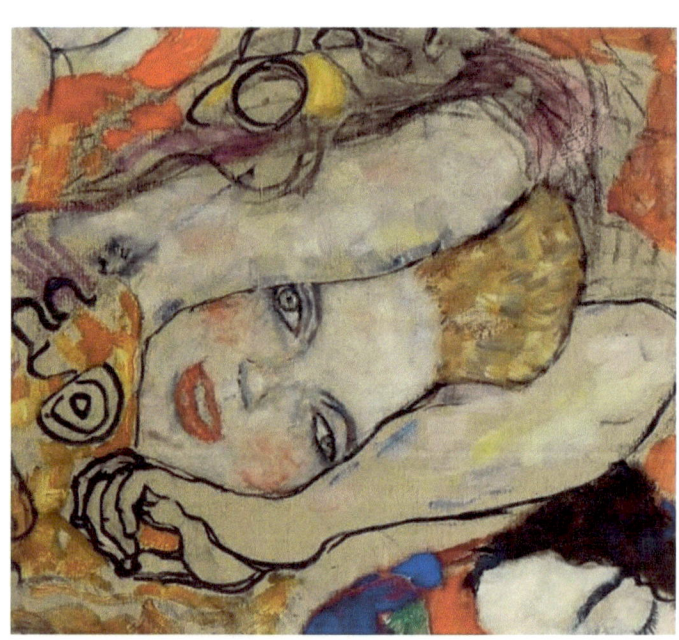

Detail

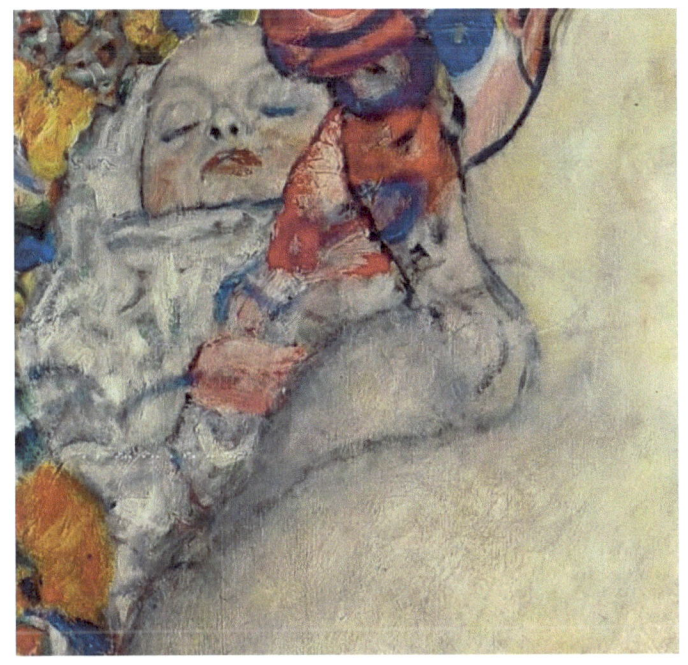

Detail

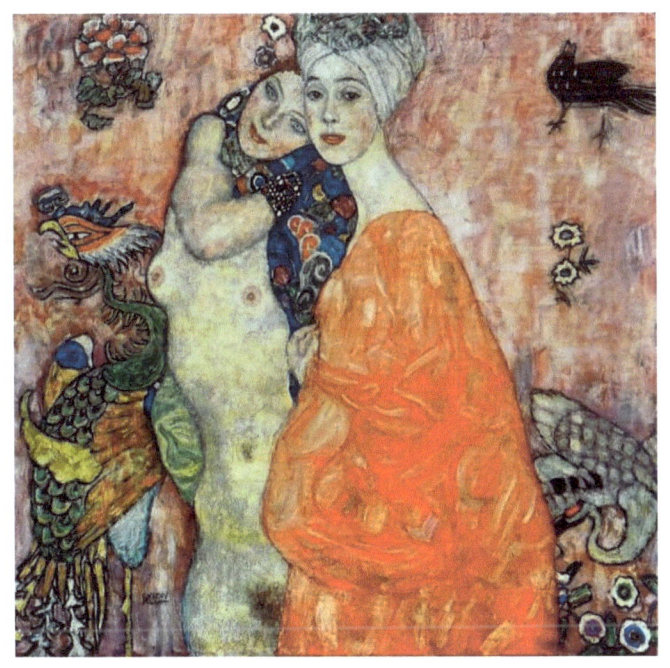

Girlfriends
1916-17, 99 x 99, destroyed by fire in 1945,
Oil on canvas

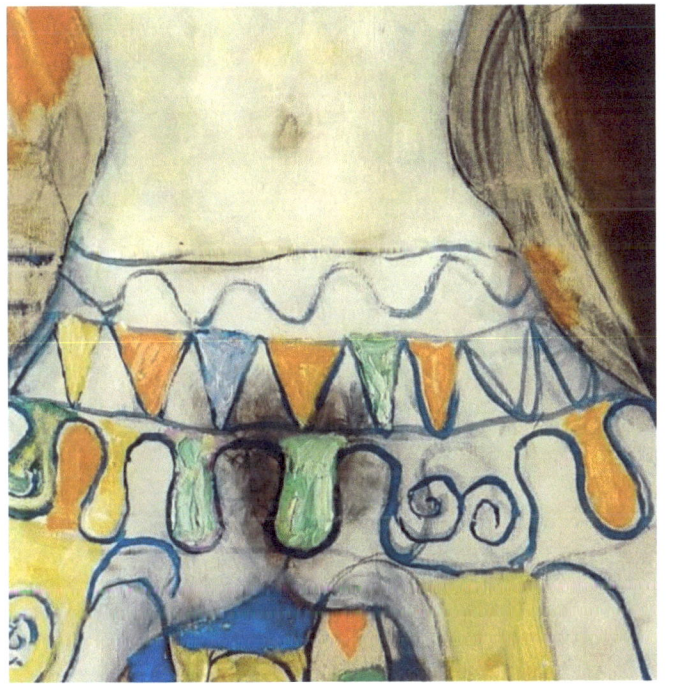

Detail

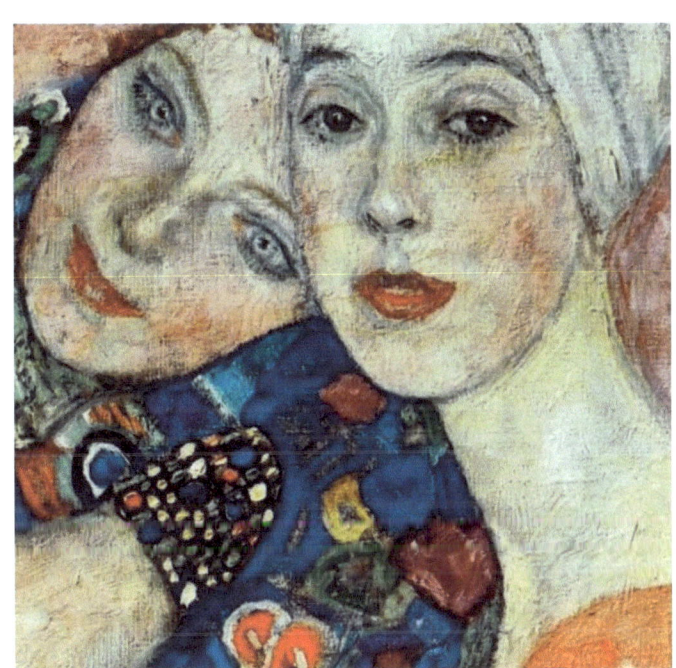

Detail

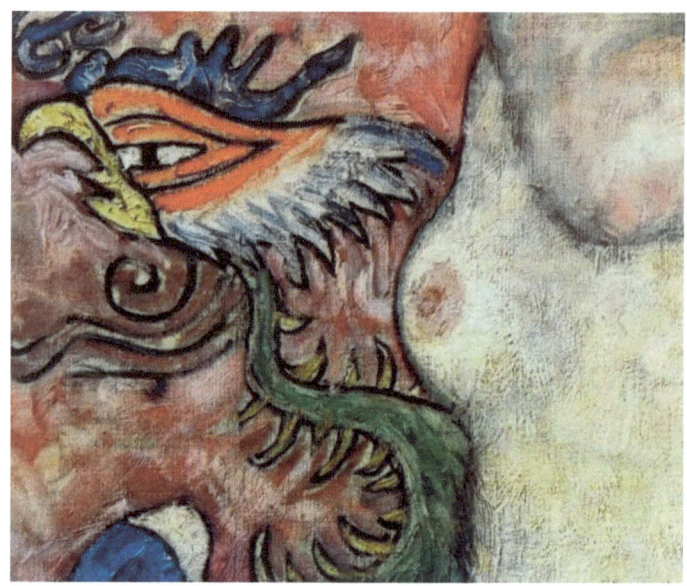

Detail

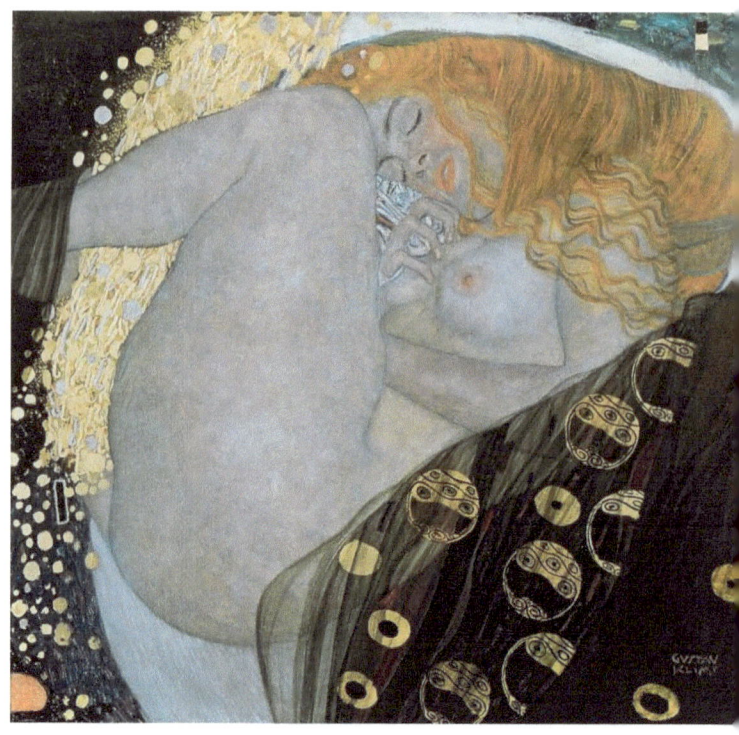

Danae
1908, oil on canvas

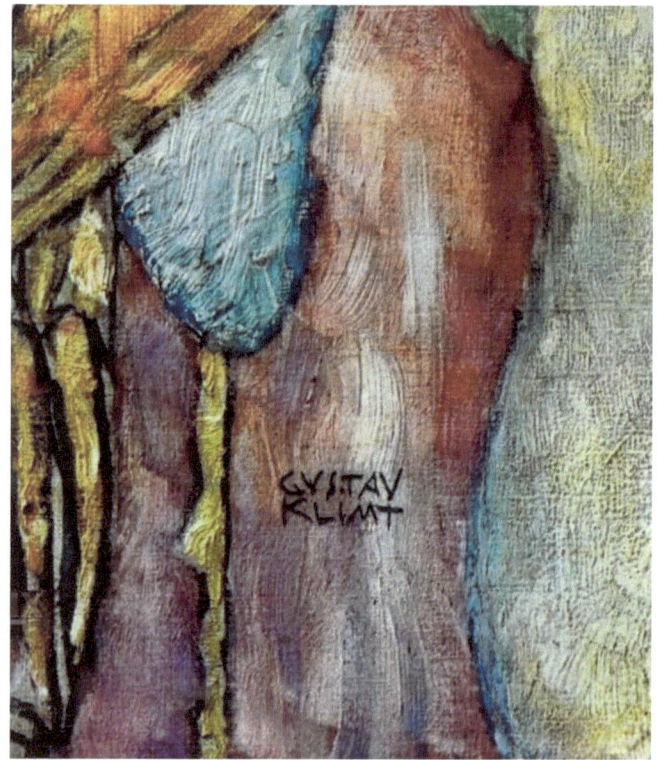

Detail

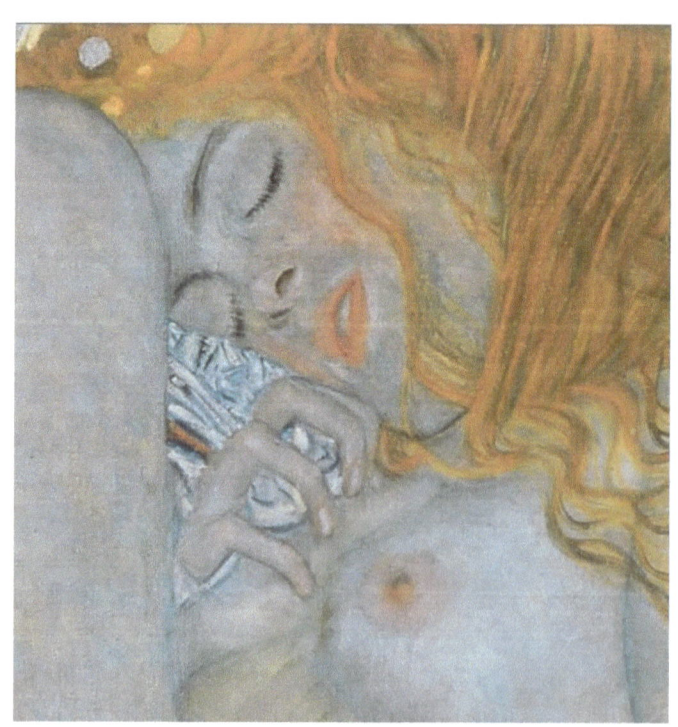

Detail

22

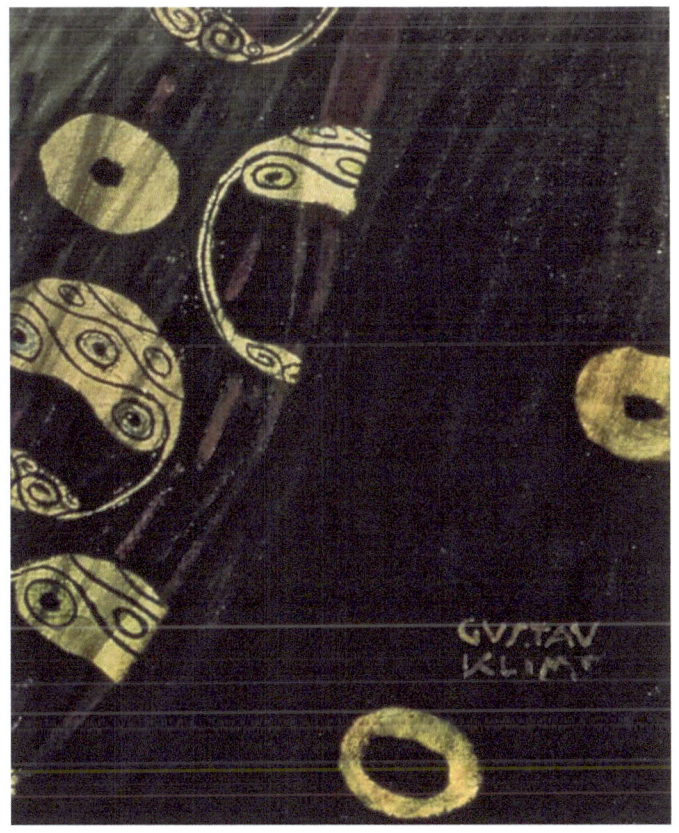

Detail

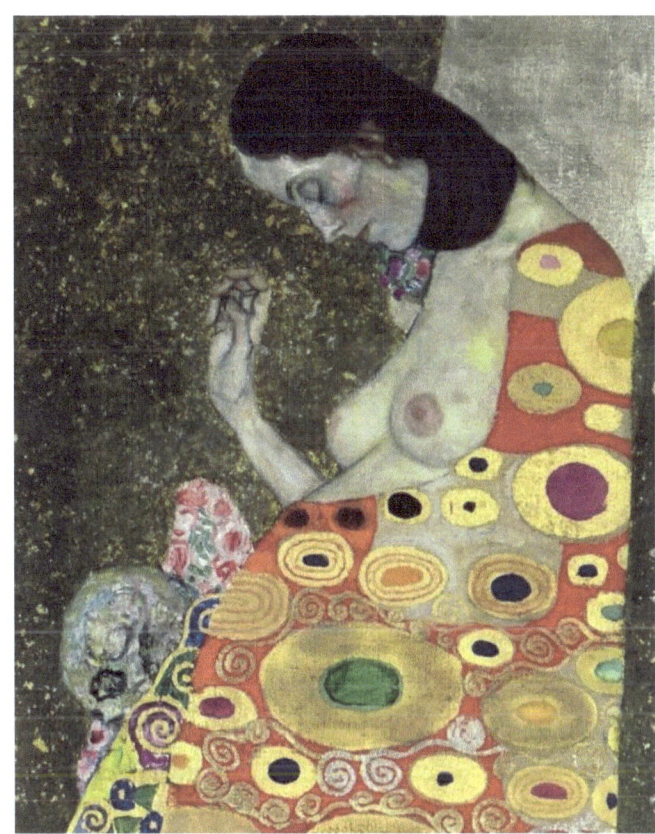

Detail

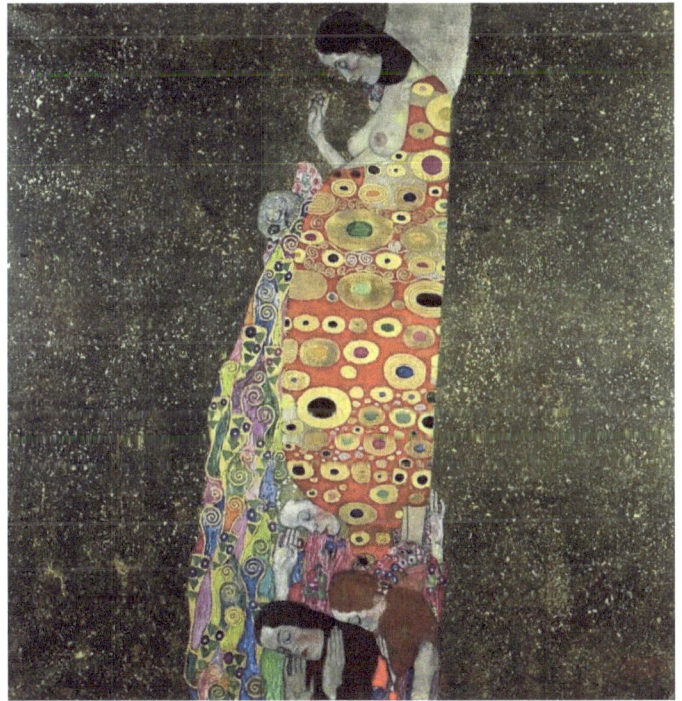

Hope II
1908, oil on canvas

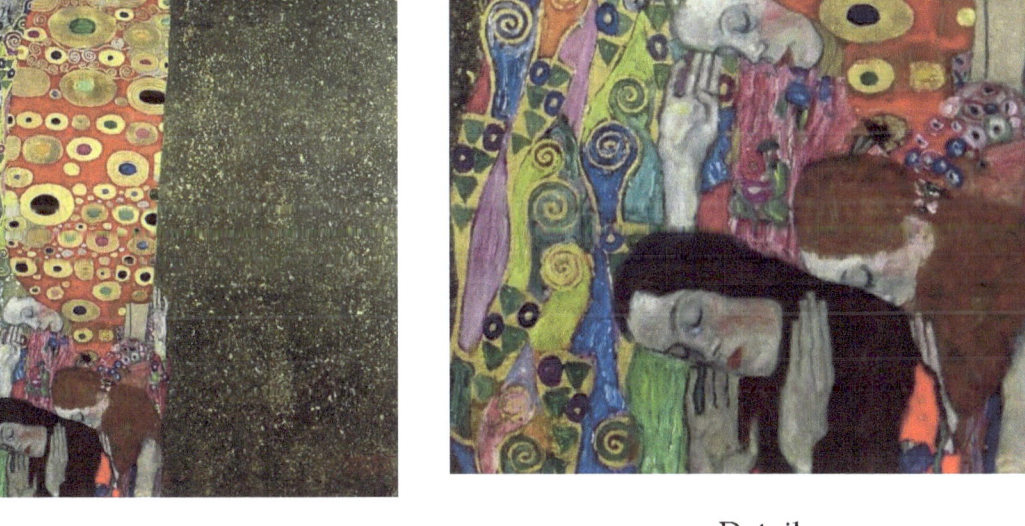

Detail

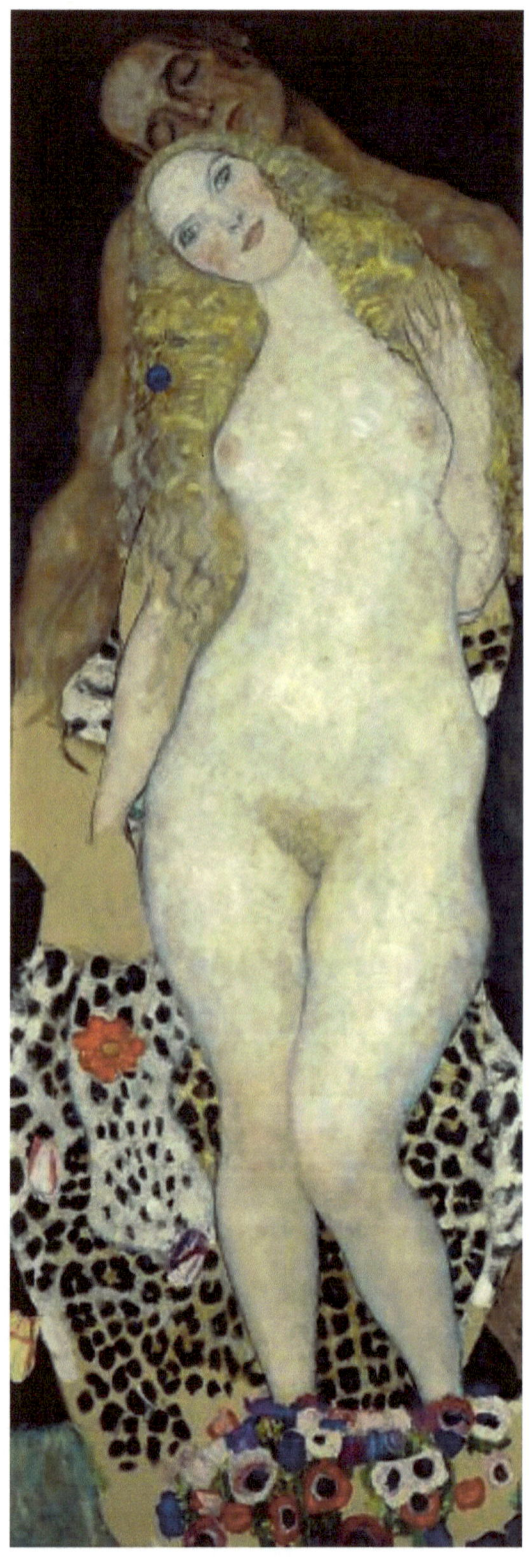

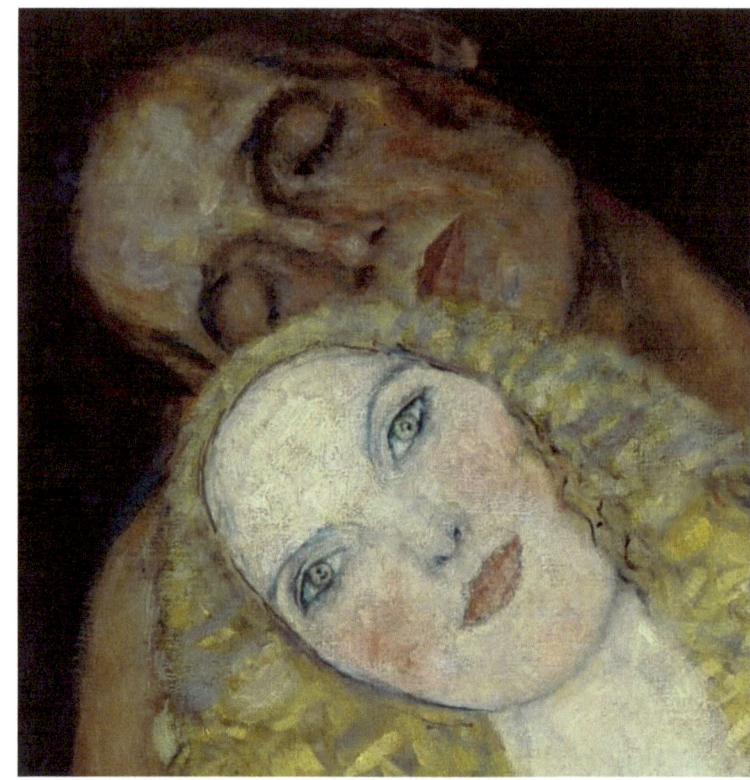

Detail

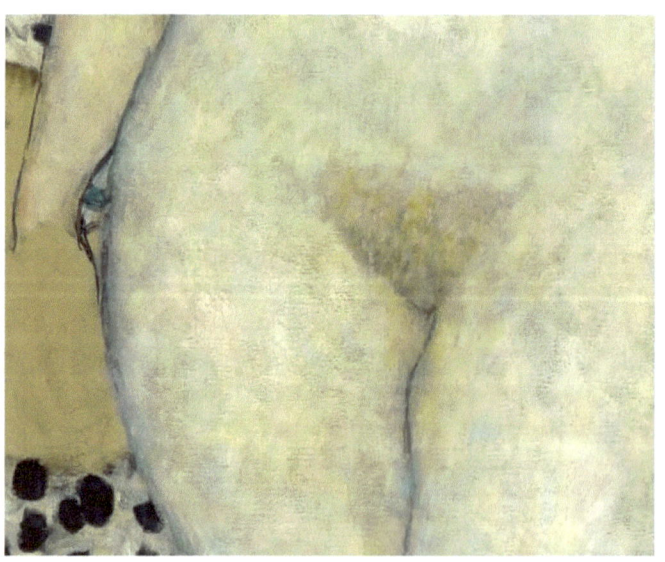

Detail

Adam and Eva (unfinished)
1918, oil on canvas

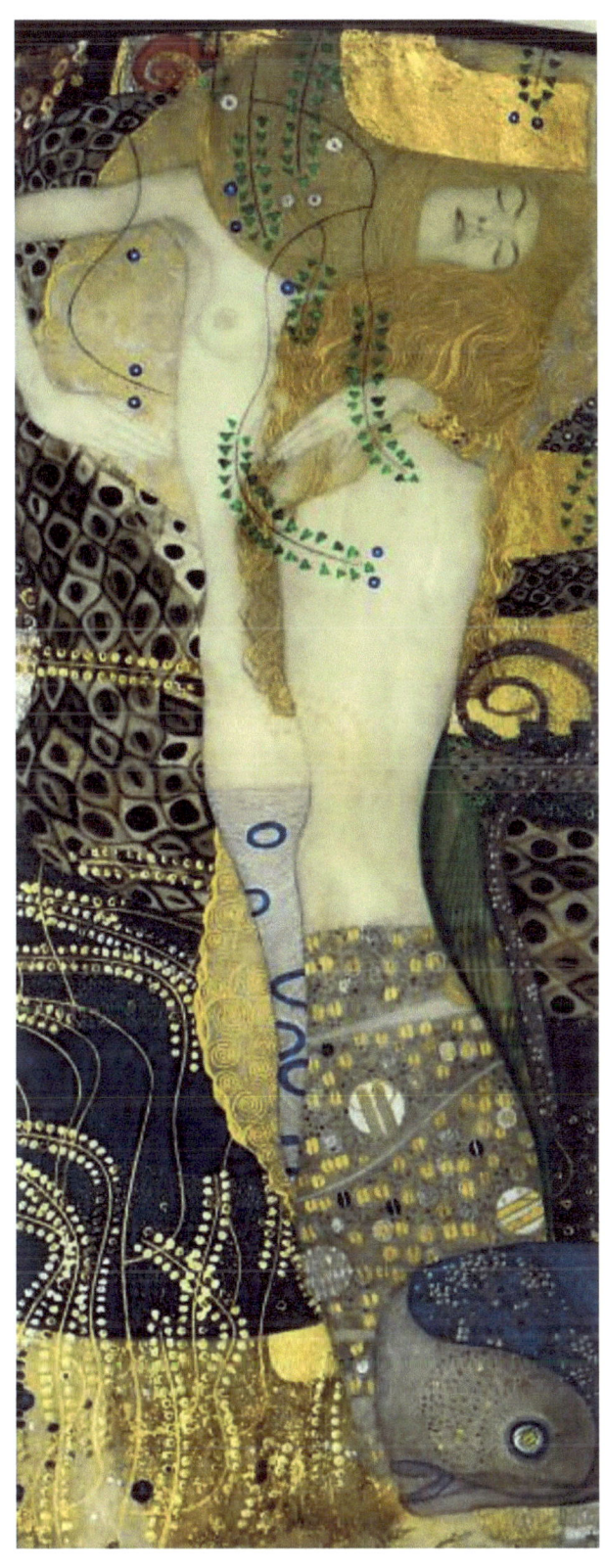

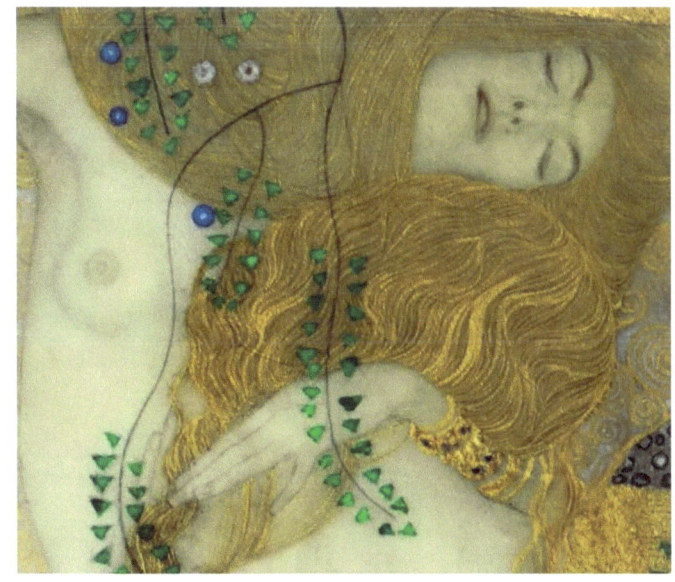

Detail

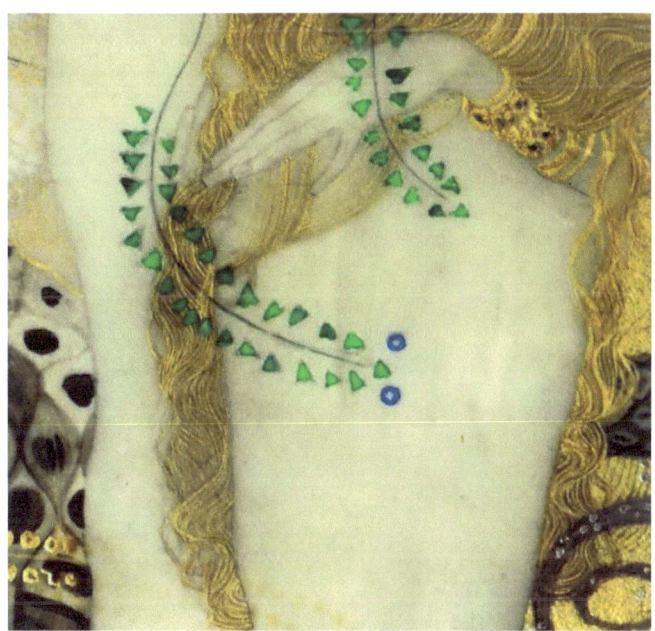

Detail

Water Serpents I
1906, Oil on canvas

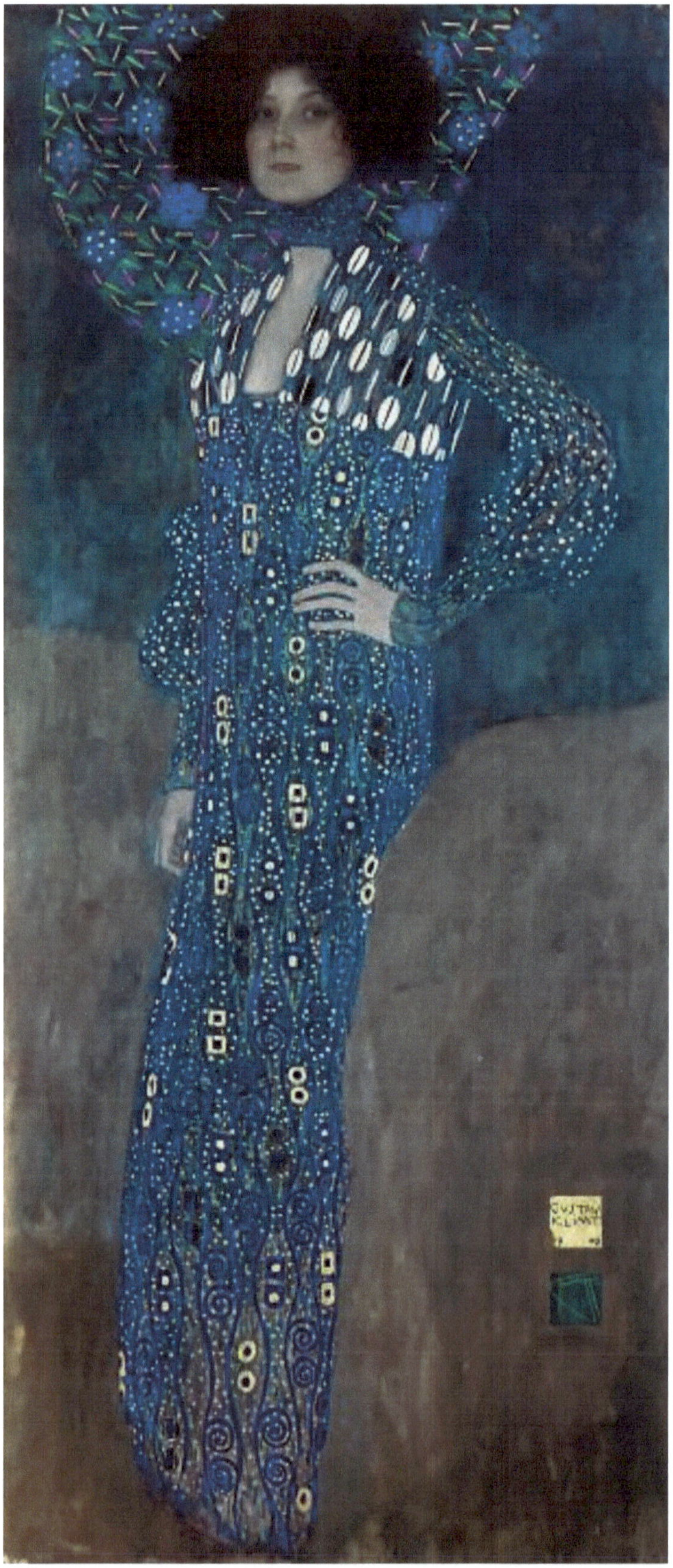

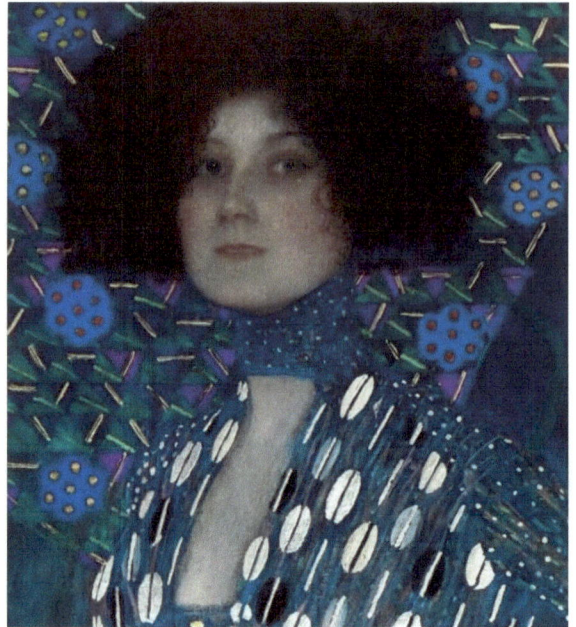

Detail

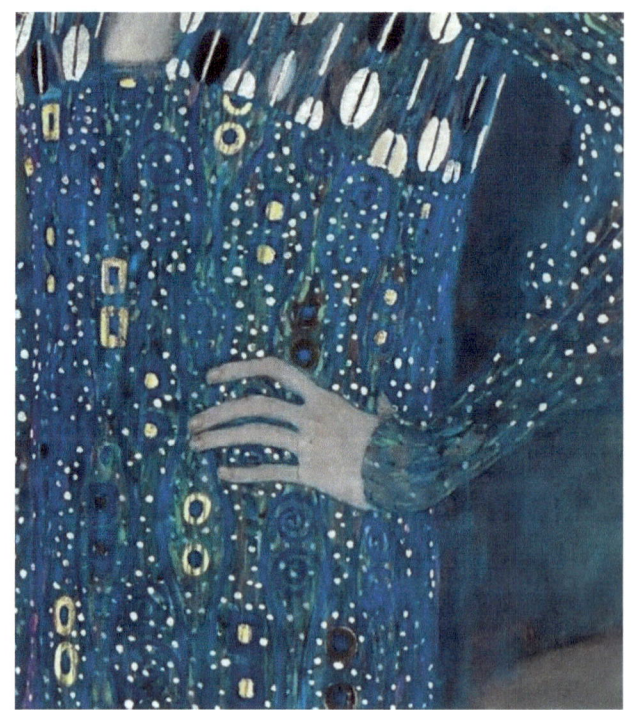

Detail

Portrait of Emilie Floge
1902, Oil on canvas, 181x84

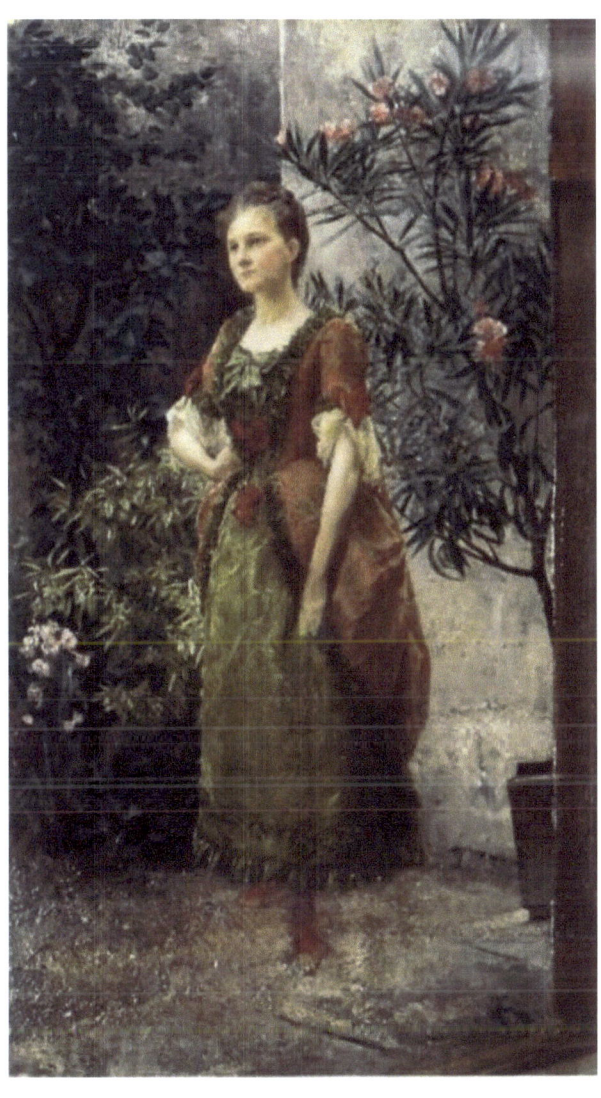

Portrait of Emile Floge
1892, oil on canvas

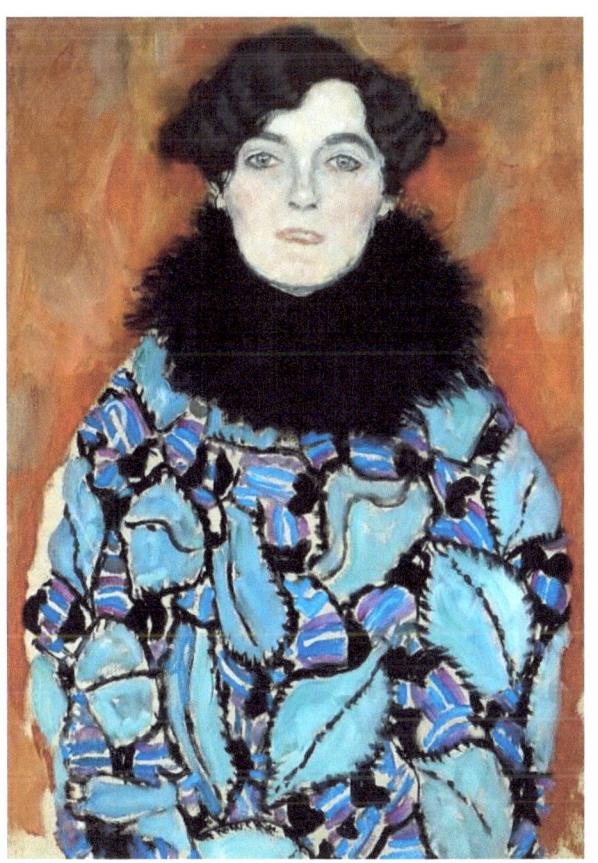

Portrait of Johanna Staude
1918, oil on canvas

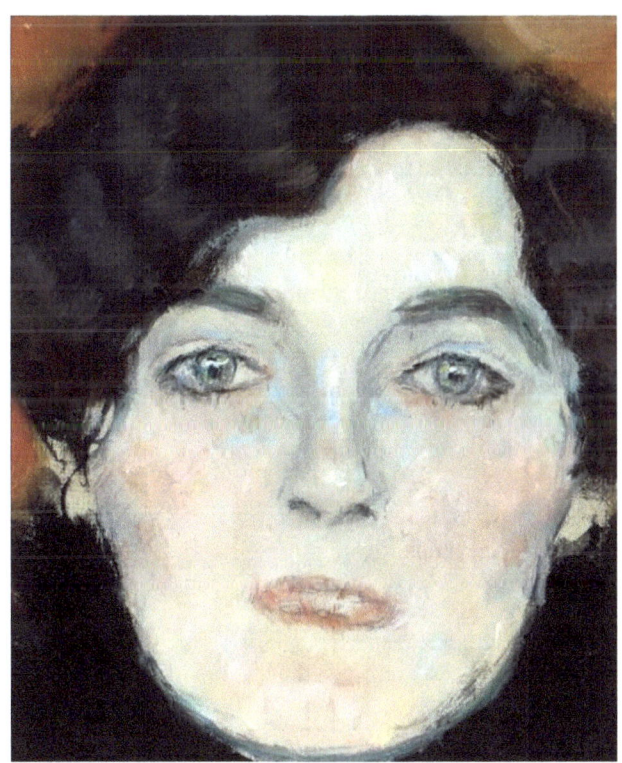

Detail

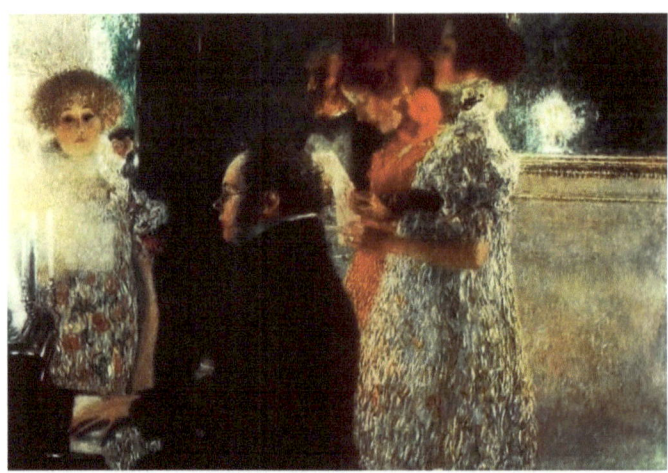

Schubert at the Piano II
1899, Oil on canvas, Destroyed during
World War II

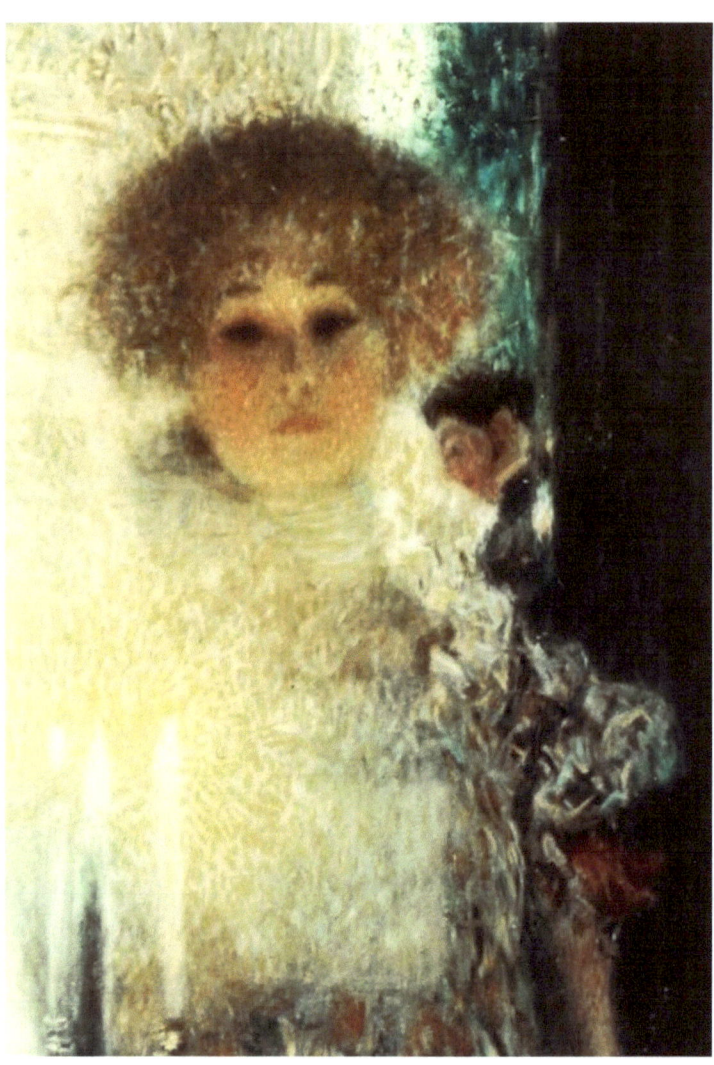

Detail

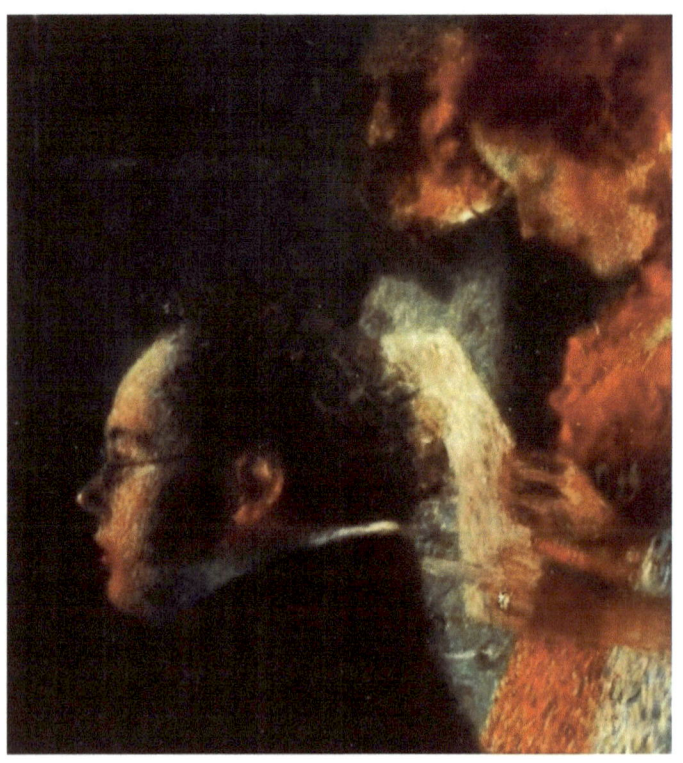

Detail

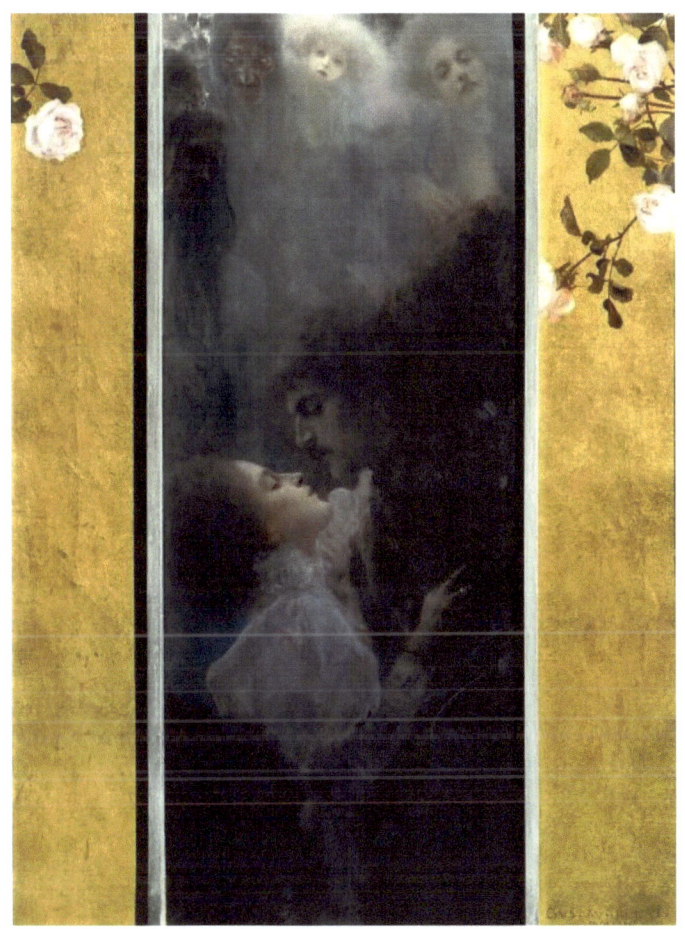

Love
1895, oil on canvas

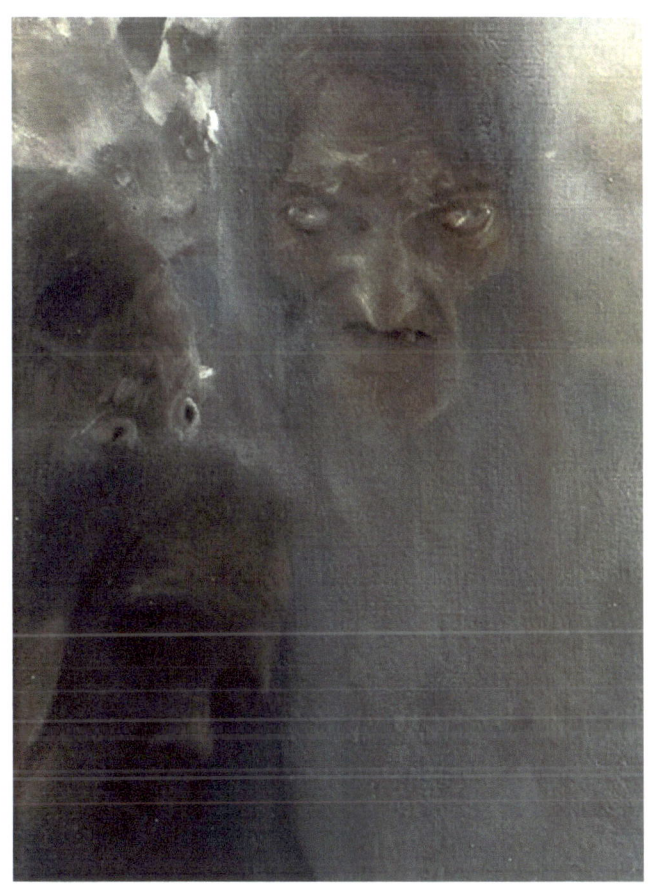

Detail

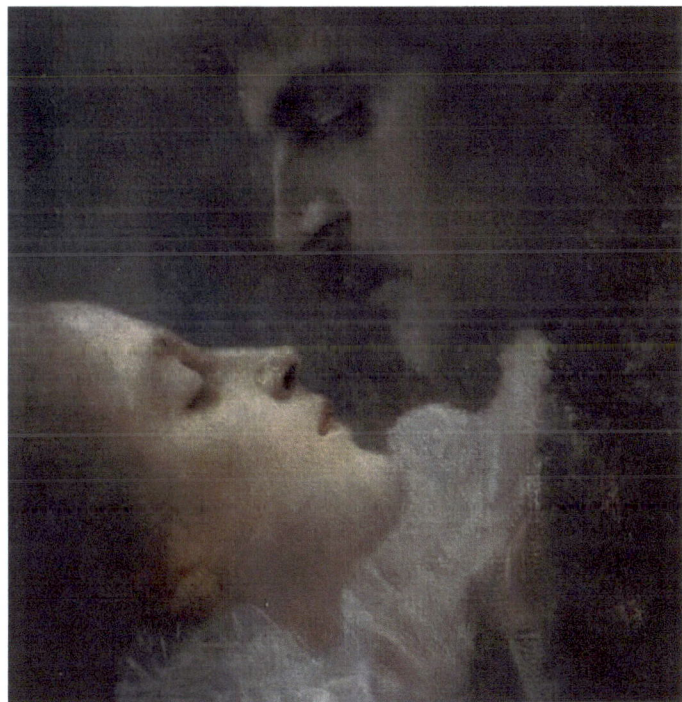

Detail

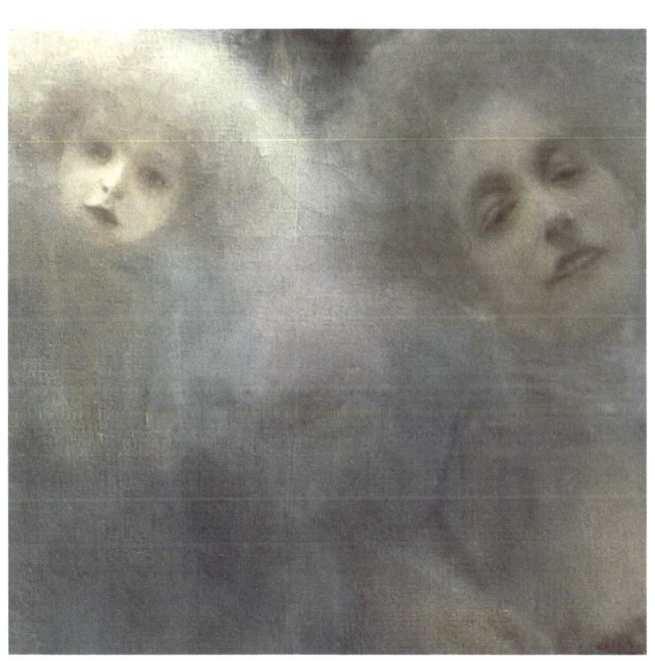

Detail

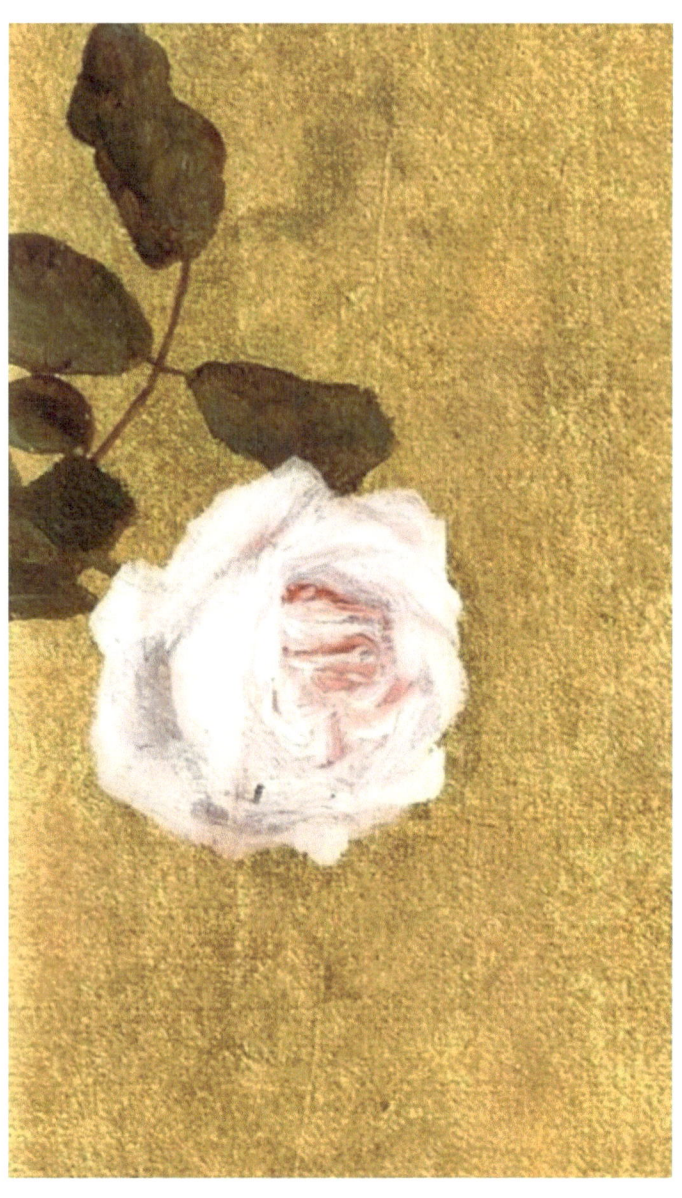

Detail

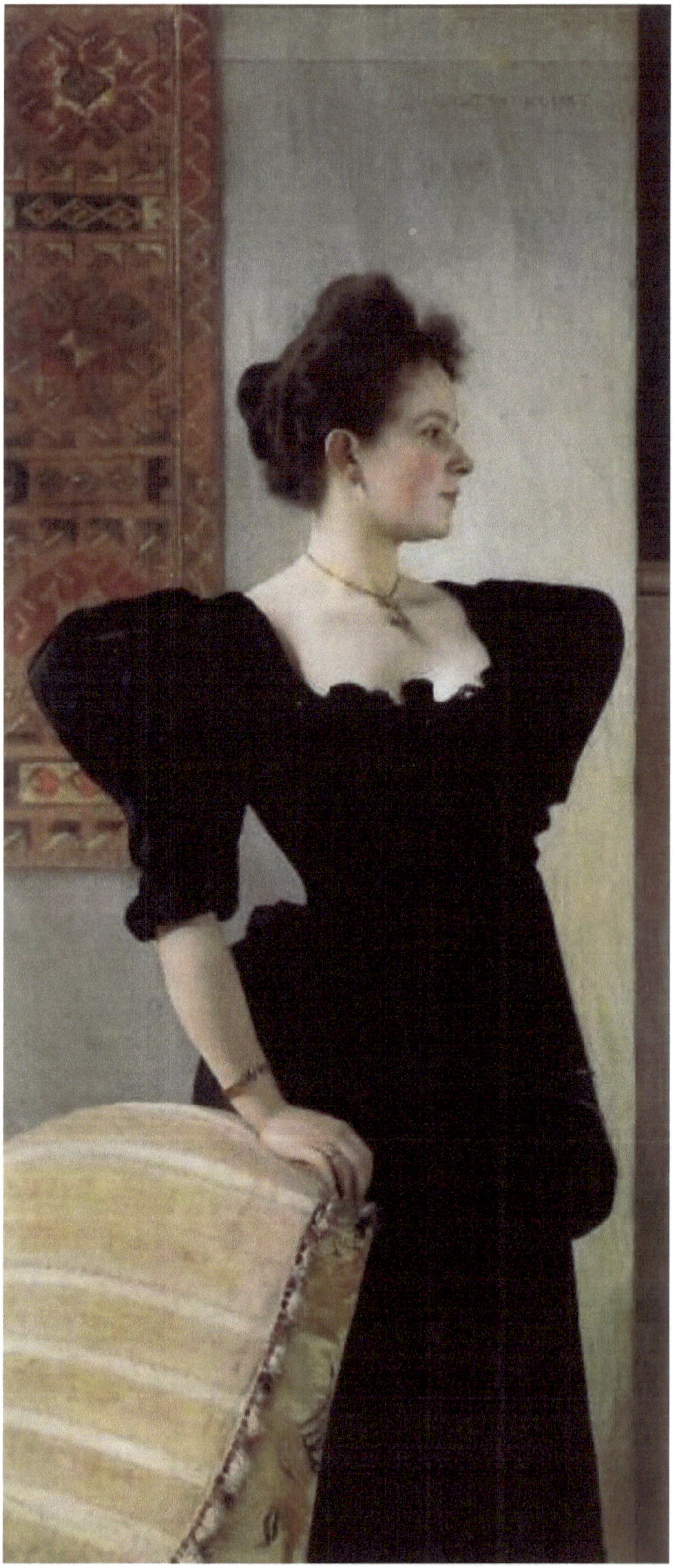

Portrait of Marie Breunig
1894, oil on canvas

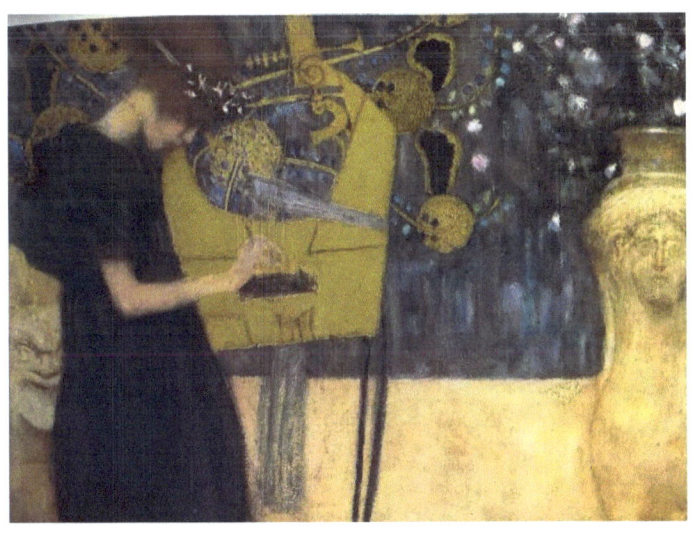

Music
1895, oil on canvas

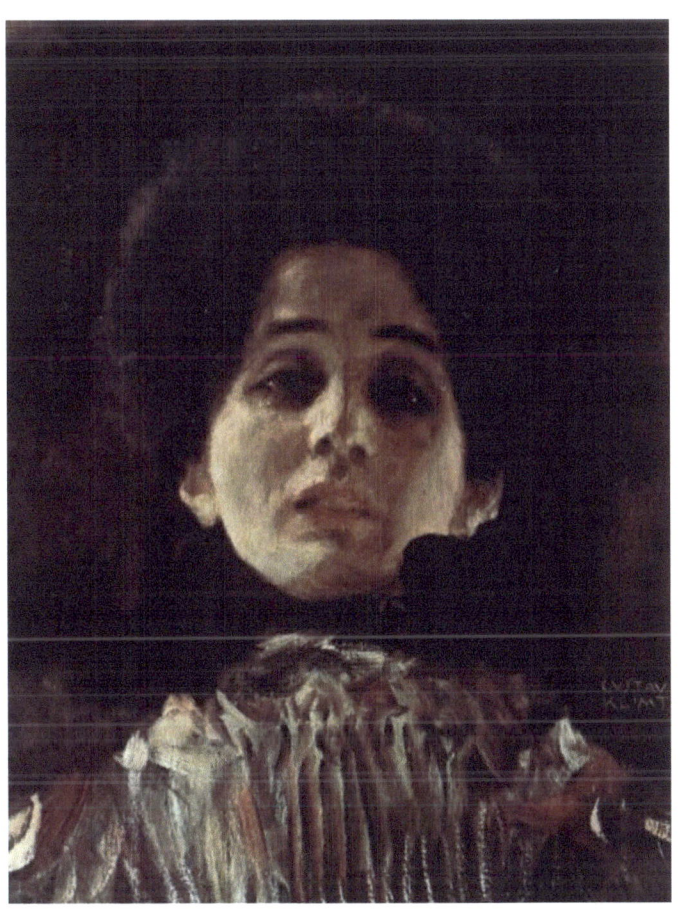

Portrait of a Woman
1899, oil on canvas

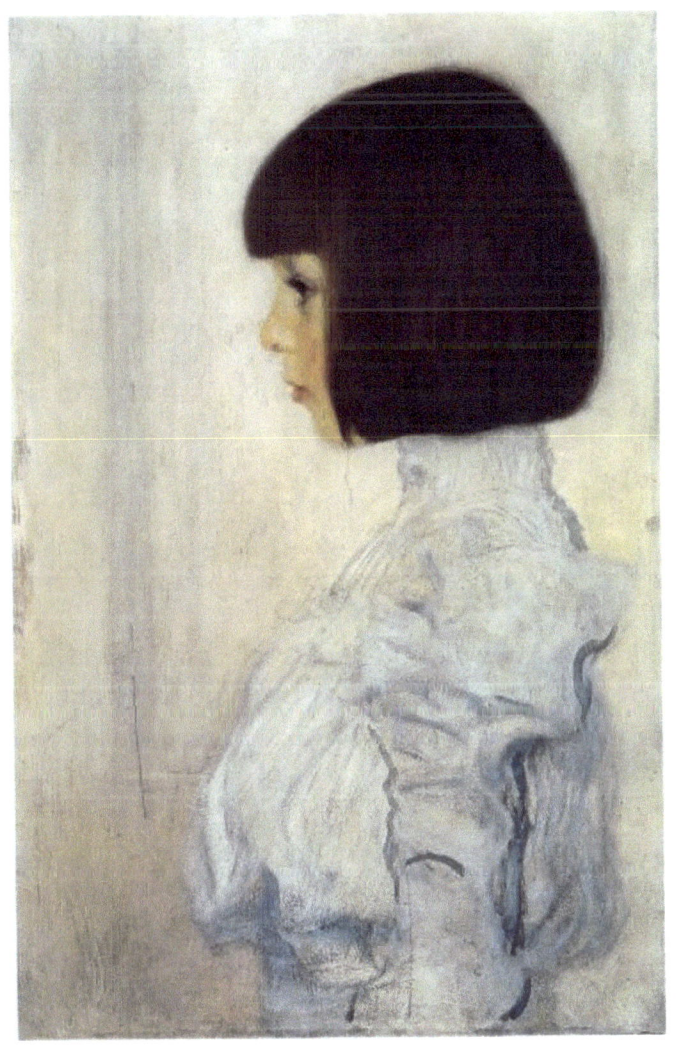

Portrait of Helene Klimt
1898, oil on canvas

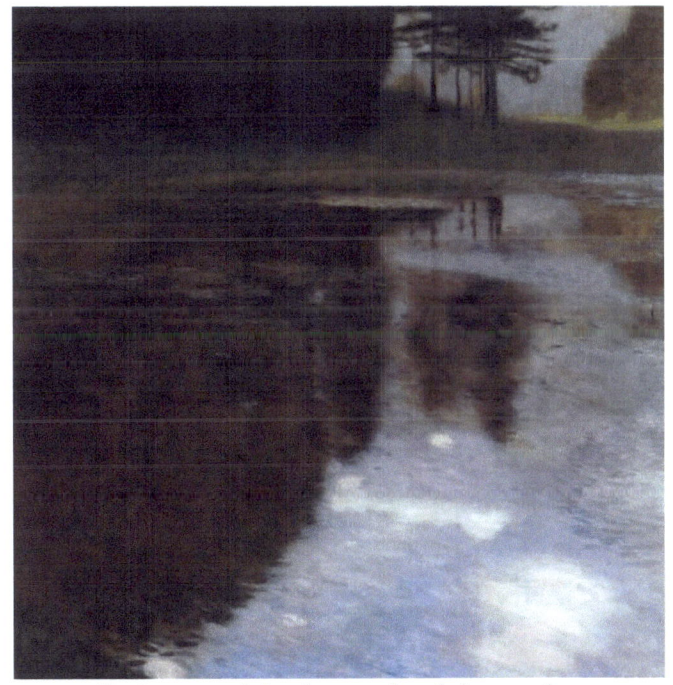

Quiet pond in the park of Appeal
1899, oil on canvas

Portrait of Serena Lederer
1899, oil on canvas

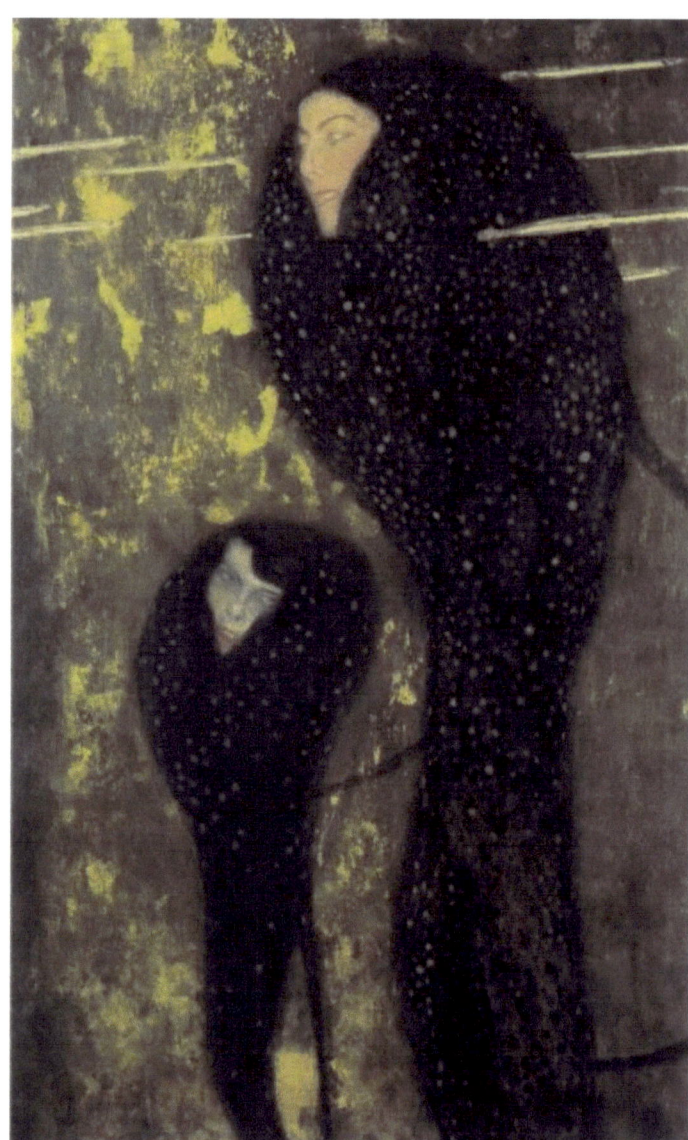

Water Nymphs (Silverfish)
1899, oil on canvas

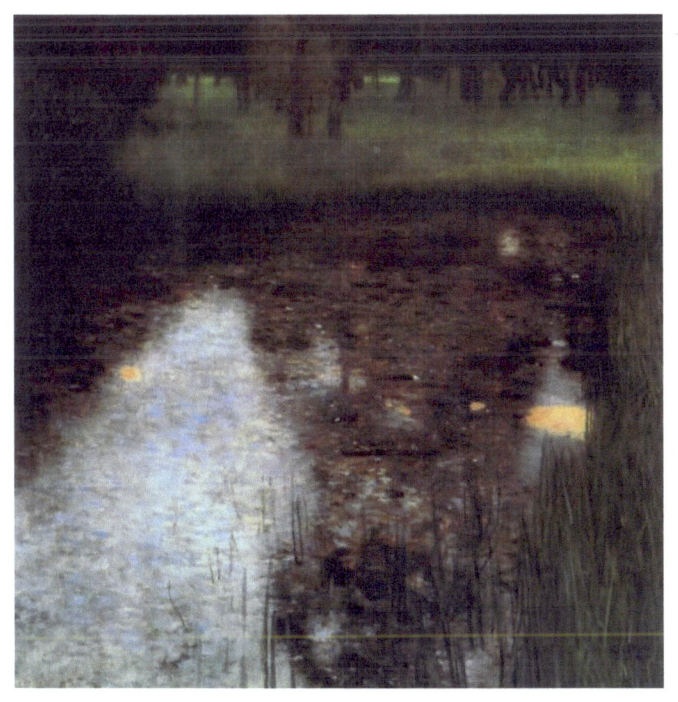

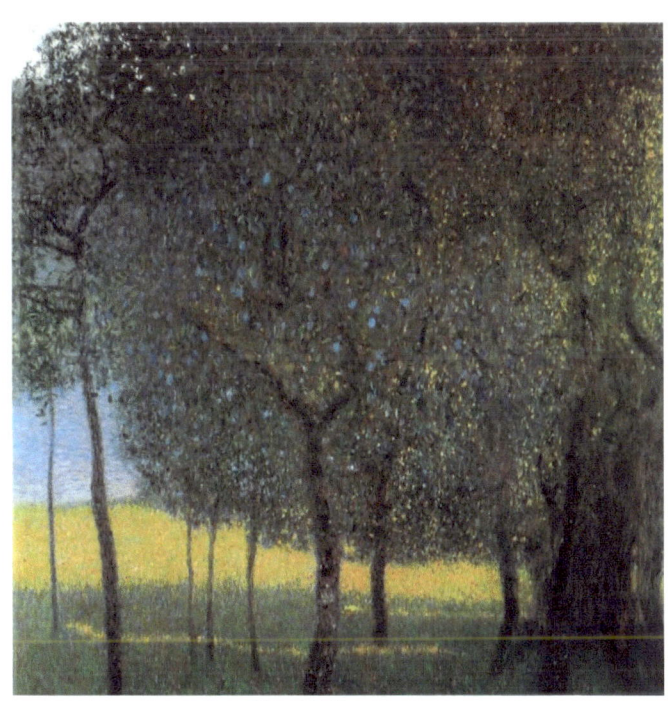

The Swamp
1900, oil on canvas

Fruit Trees
1901, oil on canvas

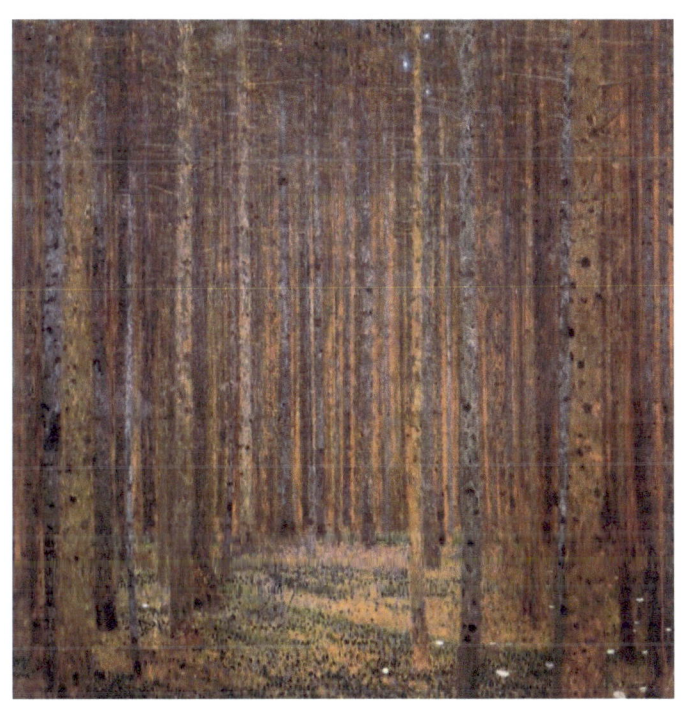

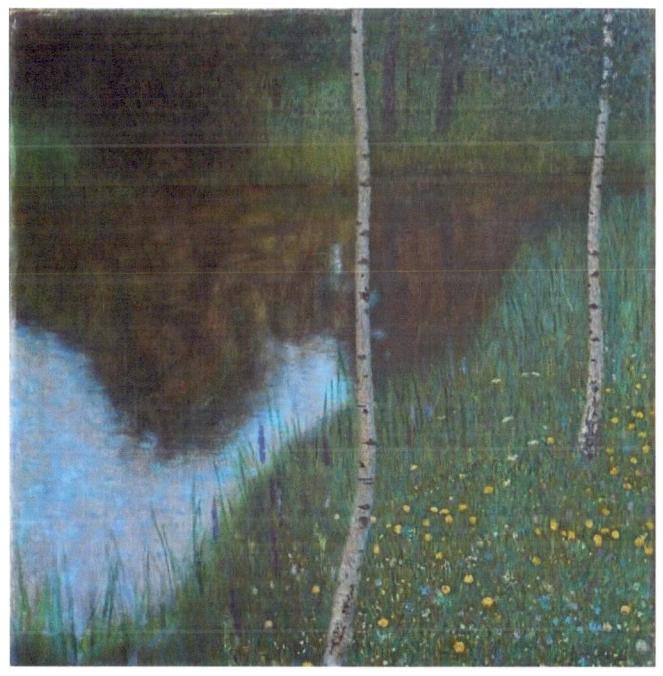

Fir Forest I
1901, oil on canvas

Lakeside with Birch Trees
1901, oil on canvas

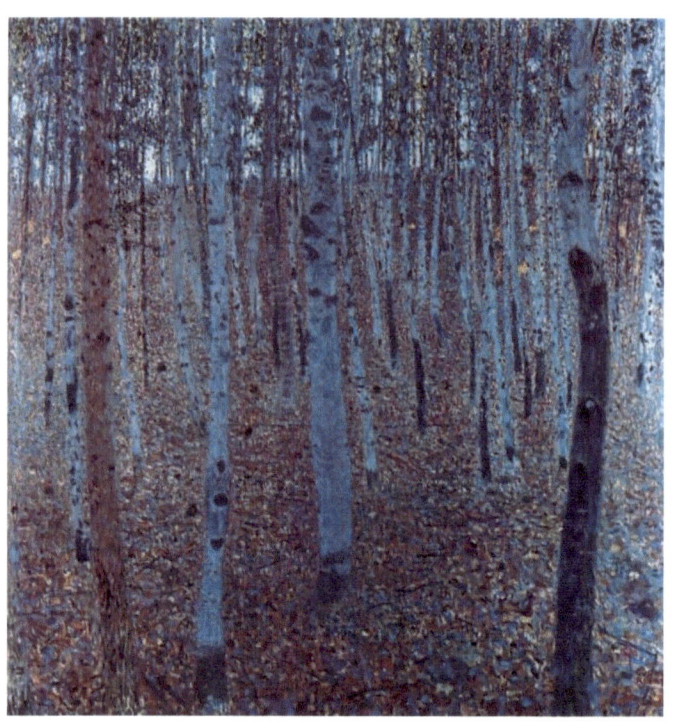

Buchenhain
1902, oil on canvas

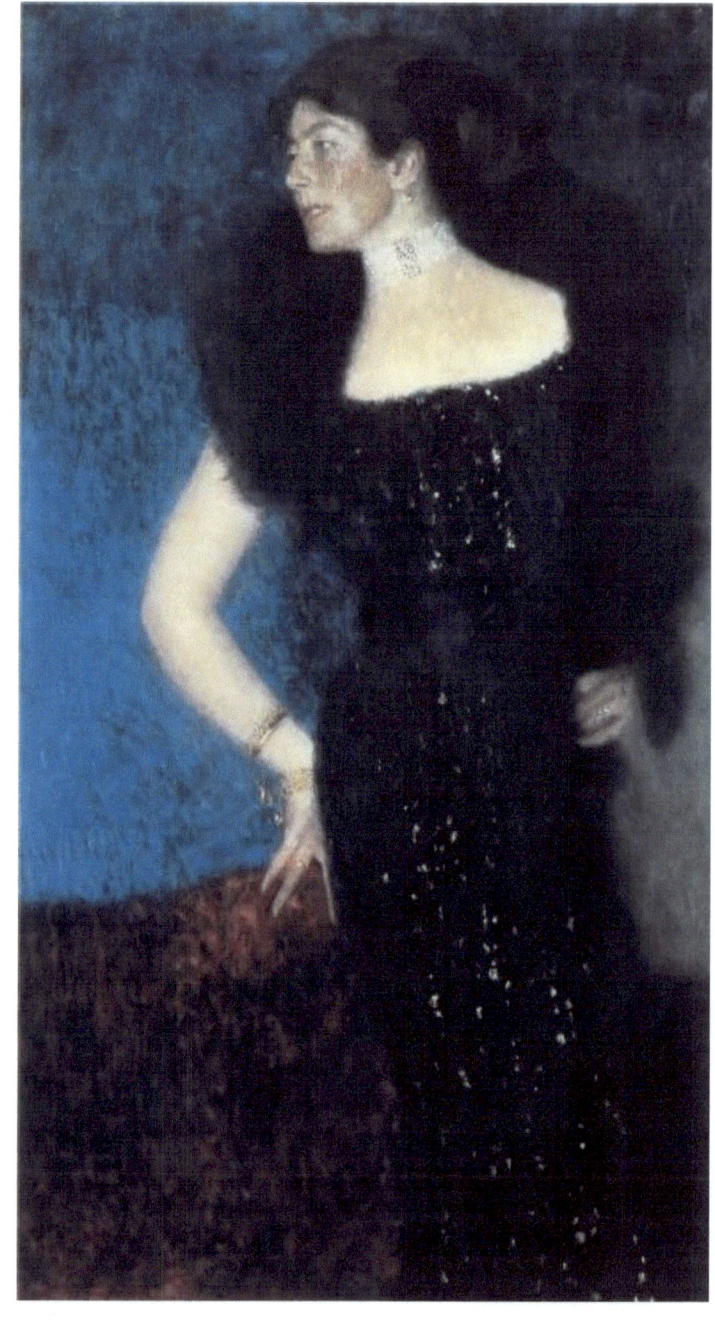

Portrait of Rose von Rosthorn-Friedmann
1901, oil on canvas

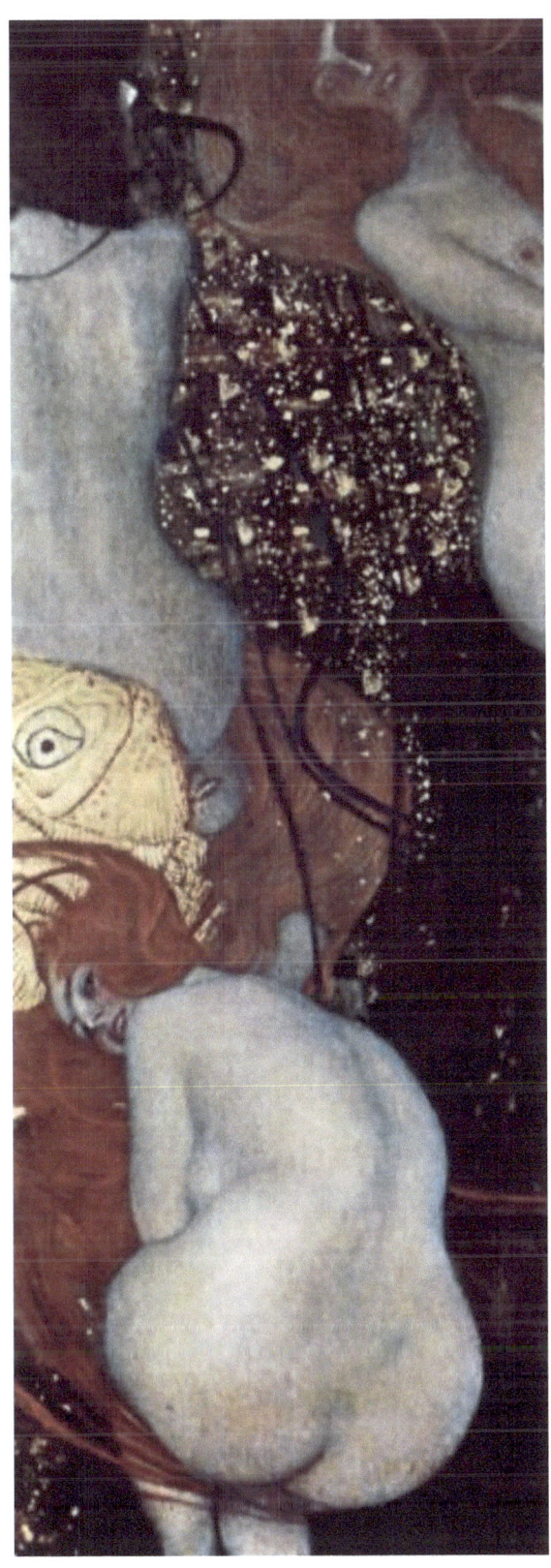

Goldfish
1902, oil on canvas

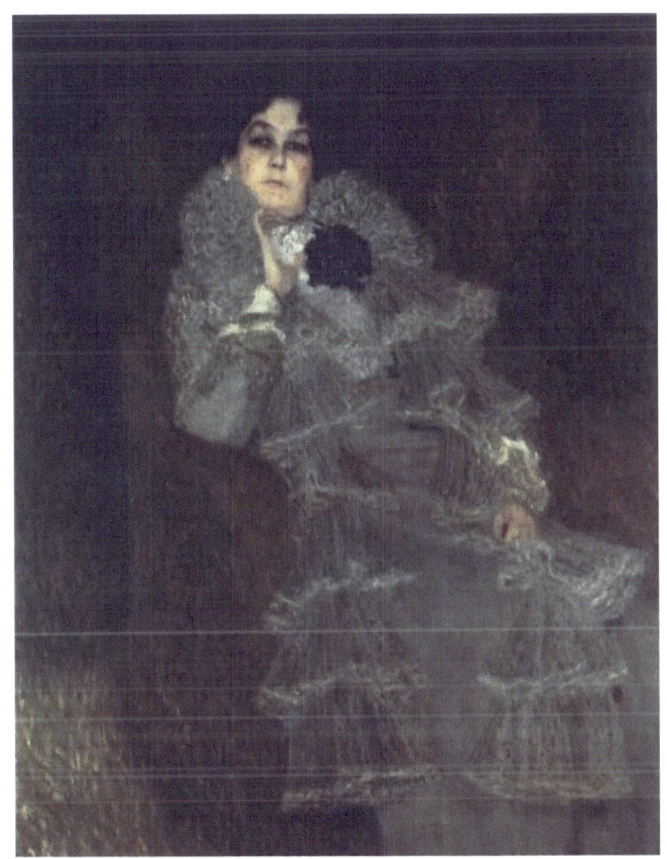

Portrait of Marie Henneberg
1902, oil on canvas

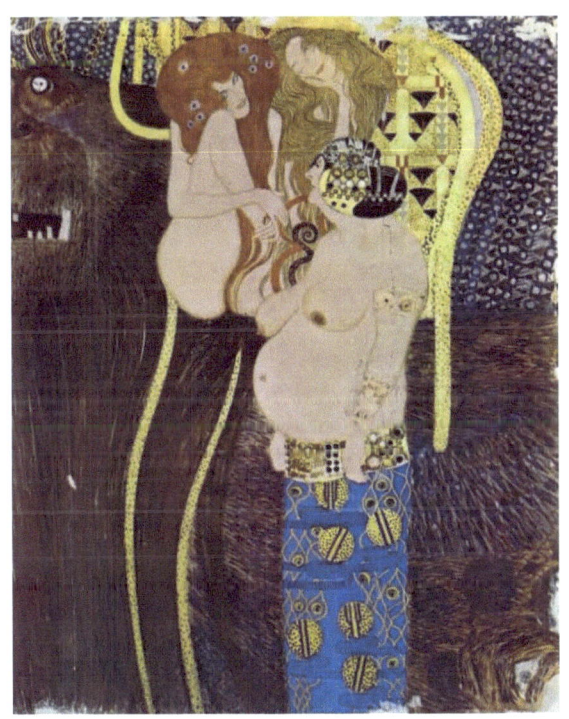

The Beethoven Frieze: The Hostile Powers.
Left part, detail
1902, oil on canvas

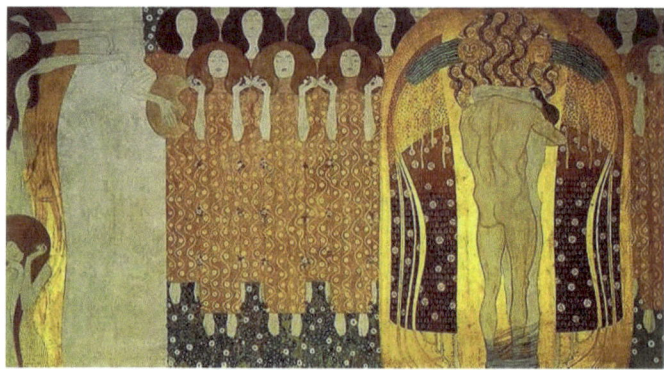

Beethoven Frieze VI, Right Wall
1902, oil on canvas

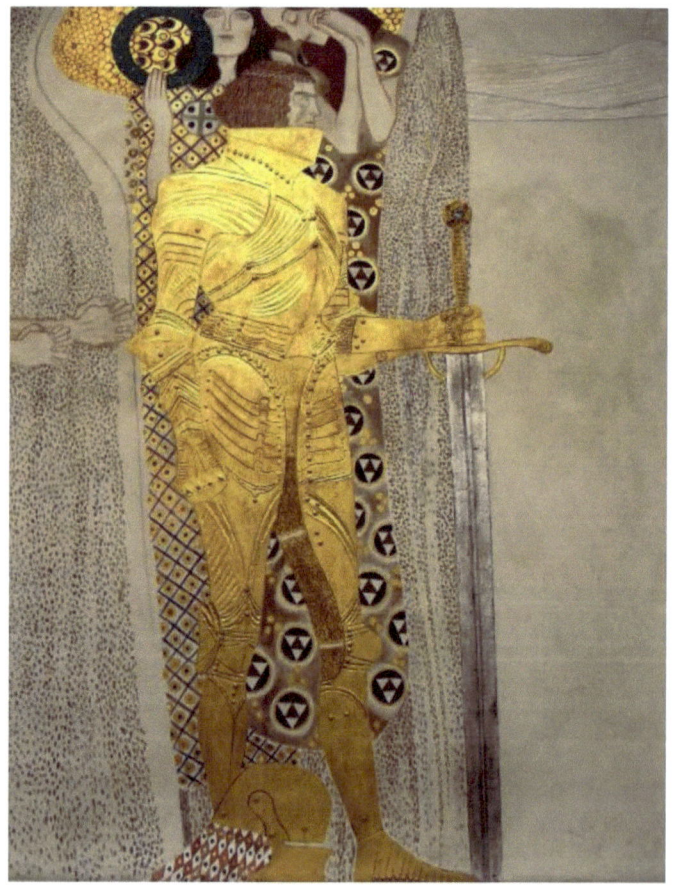

Beethoven Frieze, Knight Detail
1902, oil on canvas

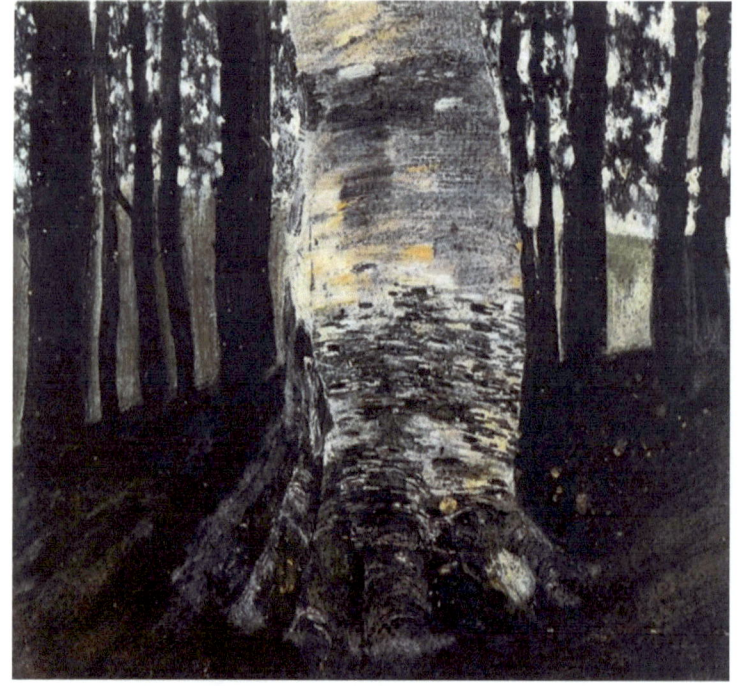

Birch in a Forest
1903, oil on canvas

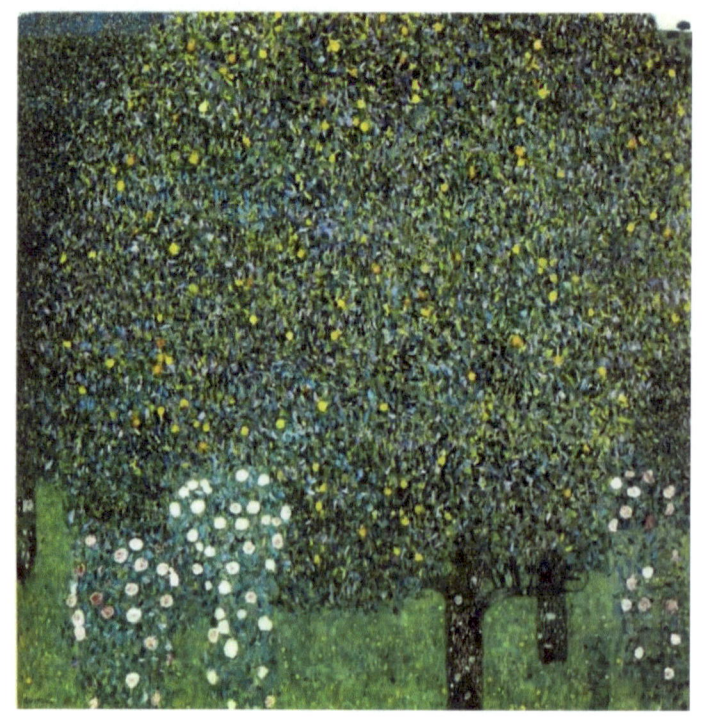

Roses under the Trees
1905, oil on canvas

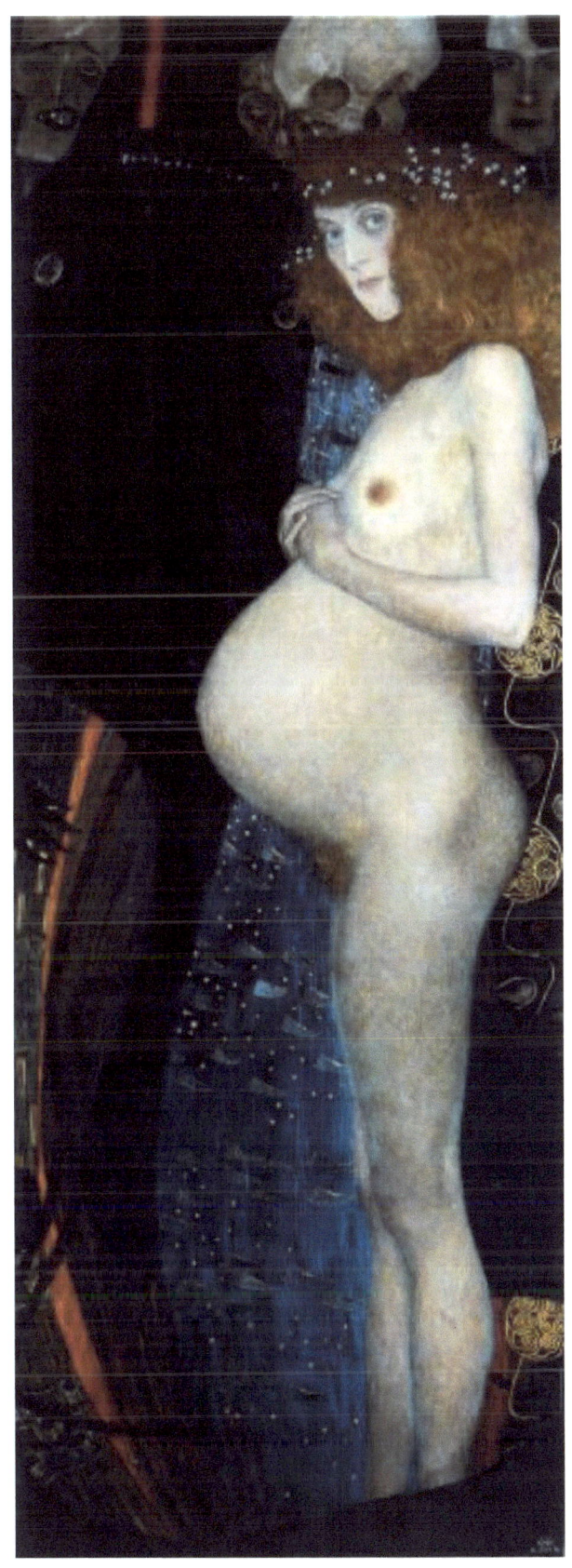

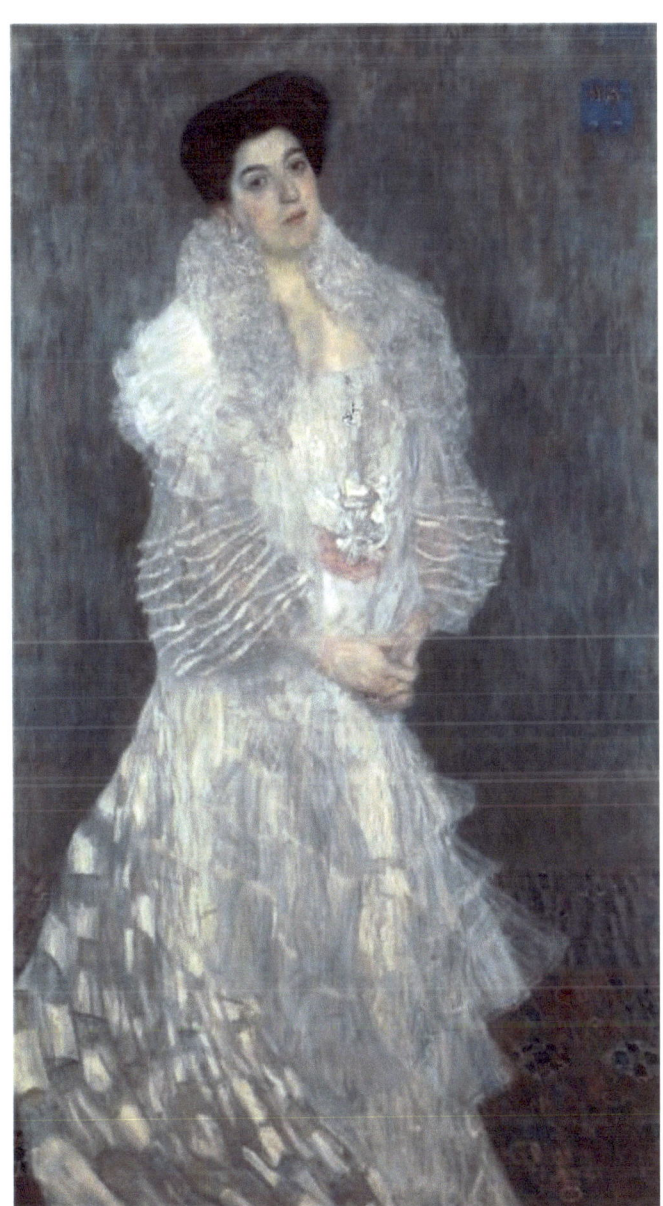

Portrait of Hermine Gallia
1904, Oil on canvas

Hope I
1903, oil on canvas

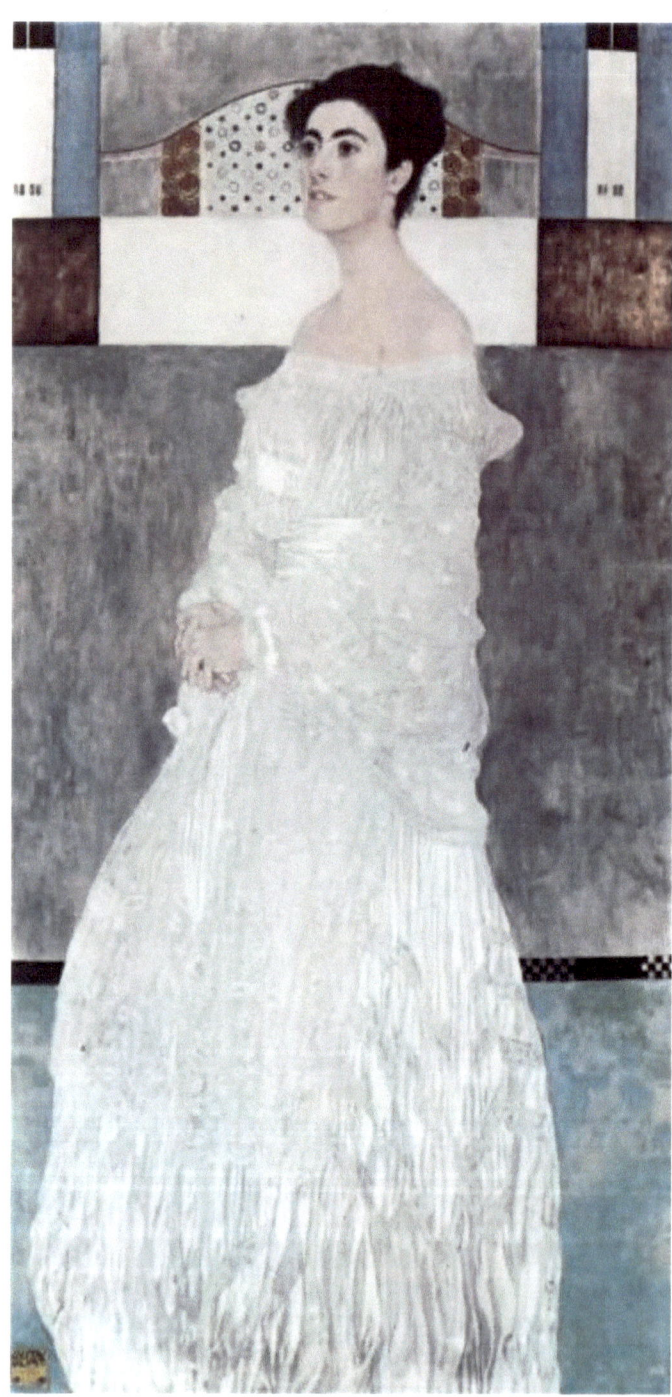

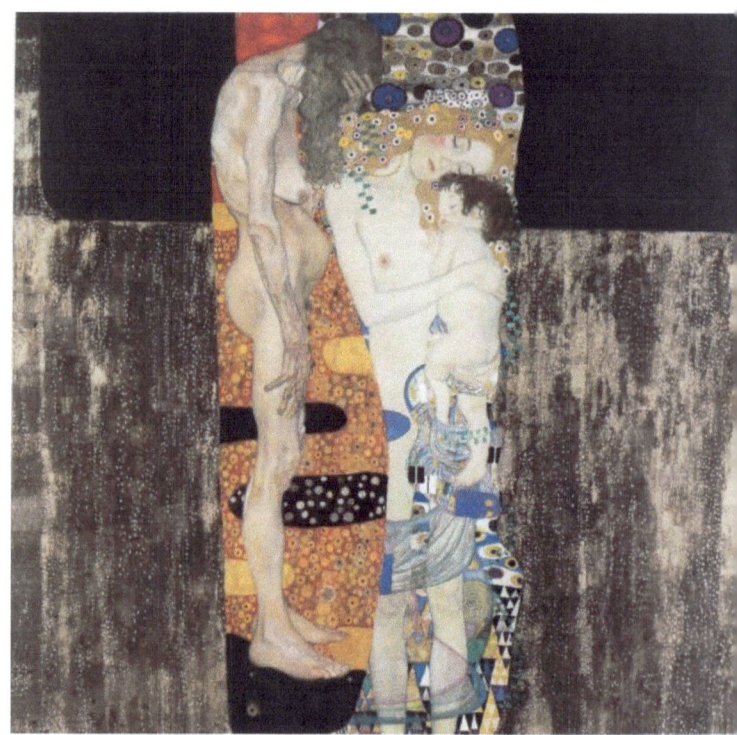

The Three Ages of Woman
1905, oil on canvas

Portrait of Margaret Stonborough-
Wittgenstein
1905, oil on canvas

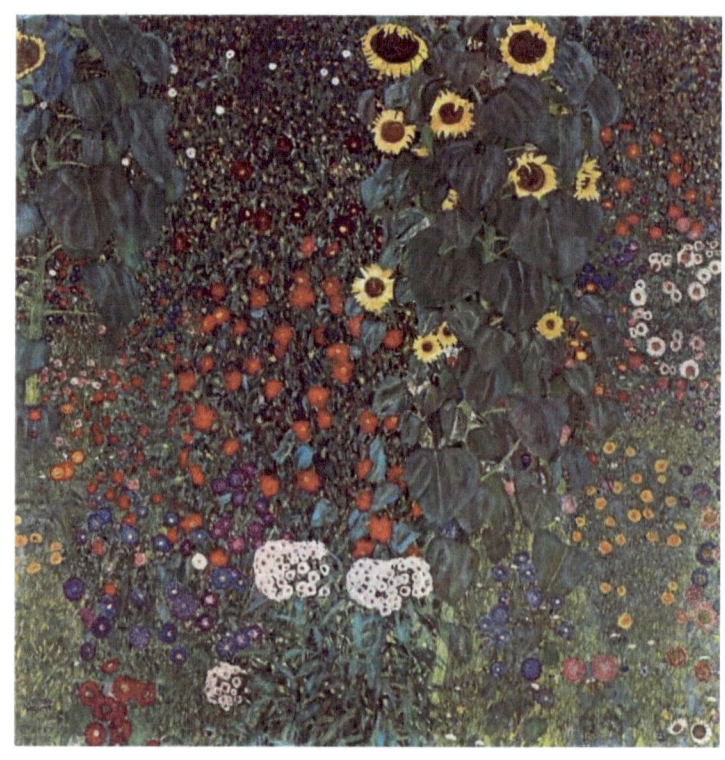

Country Garden with Sunflowers
1906, oil on canvas

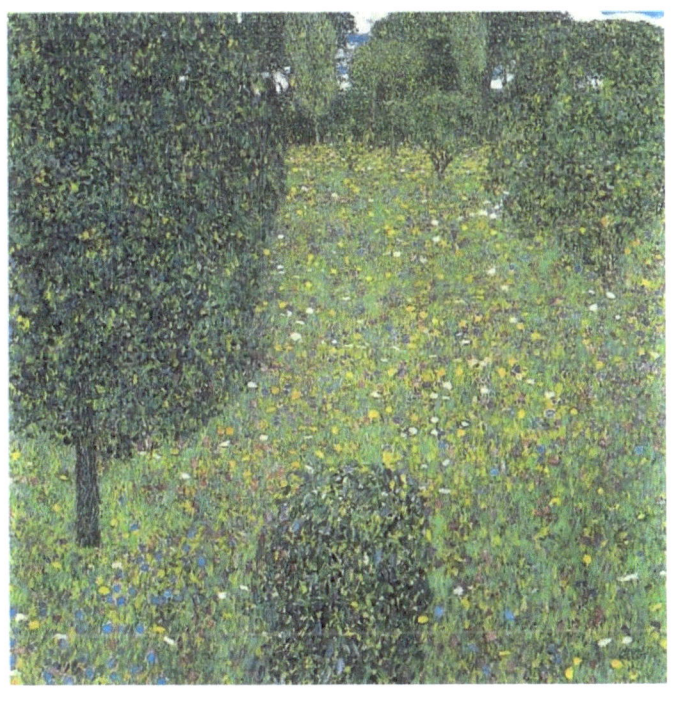

Landscape Garden (Meadow in Flower)
1906, oil on canvas

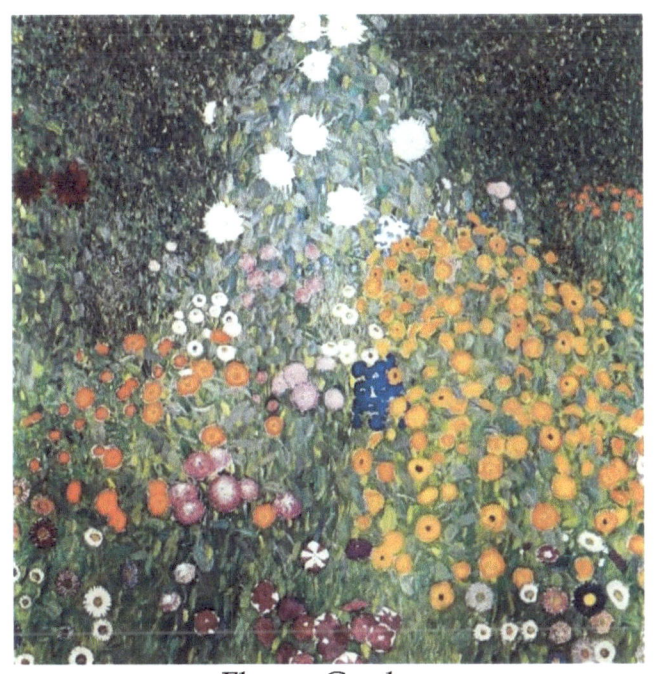

Flower Garden
1907, oil on canvas

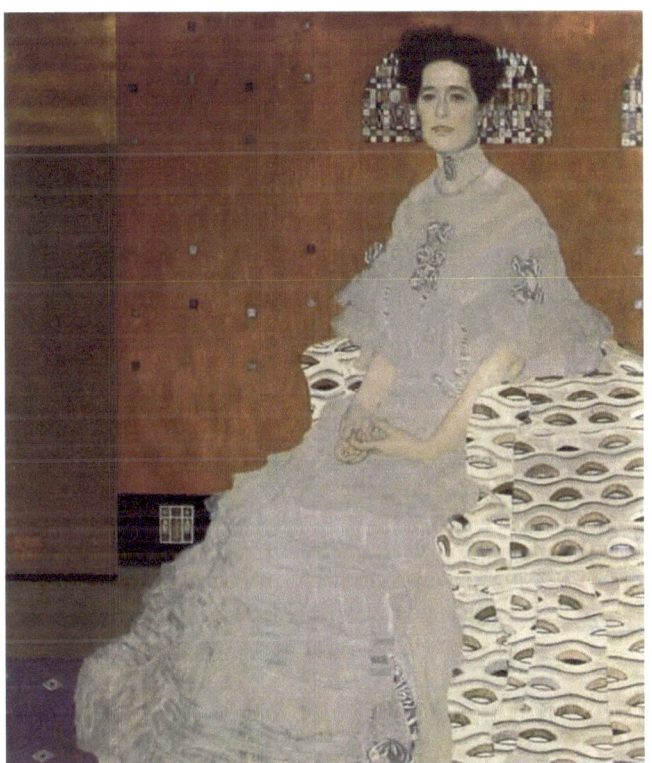

Portrait of Fritza Riedler
1906, oil on canvas

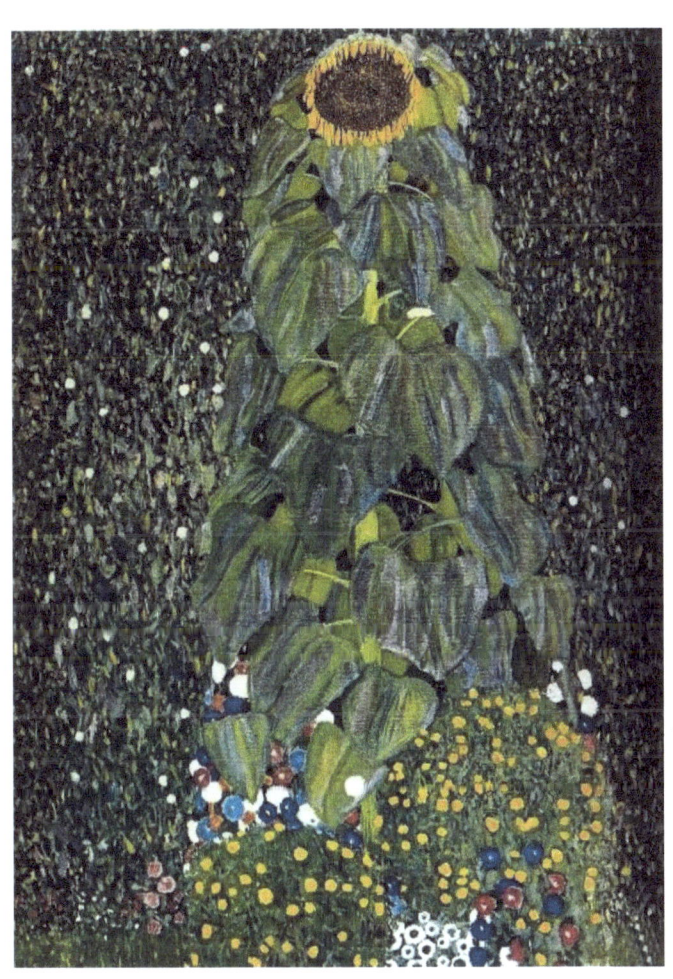

The Sunflower
1907, oil on canvas

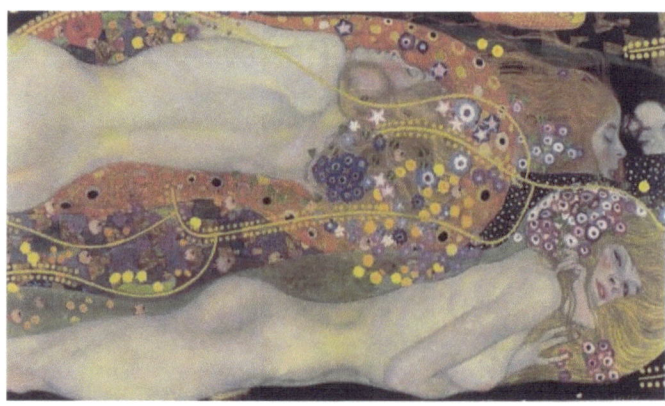

Water Snakes II
1907, oil on canvas

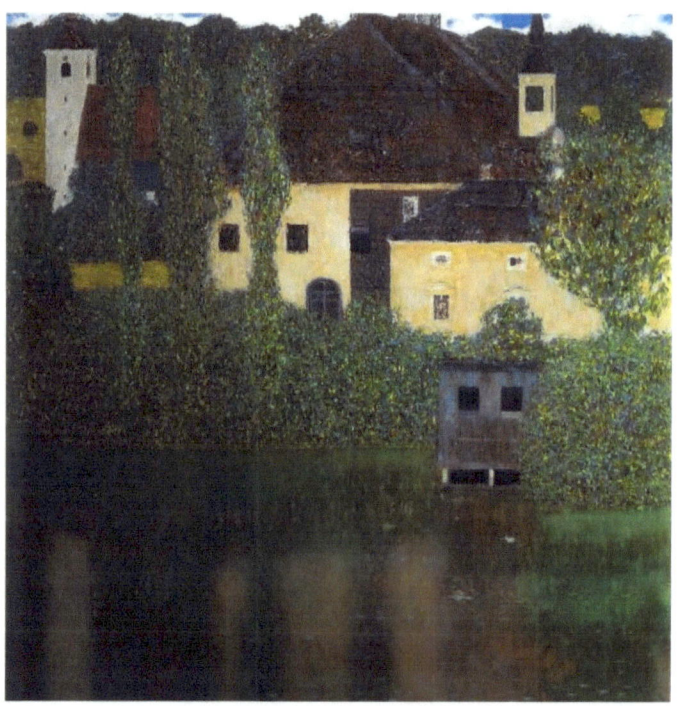

Water Castle
1908, oil on canvas

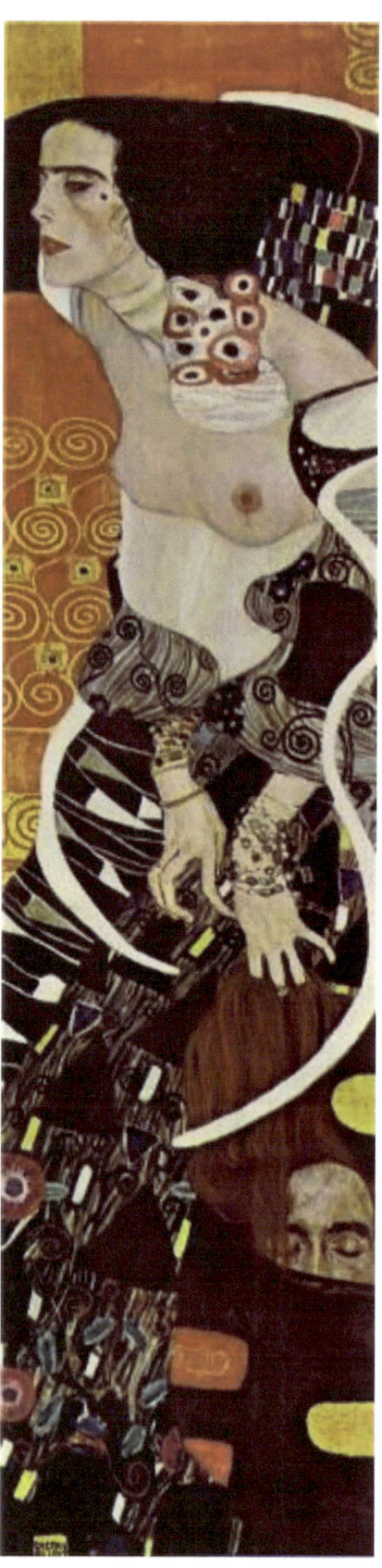

Judith II (Salome)
1909, oil on canvas

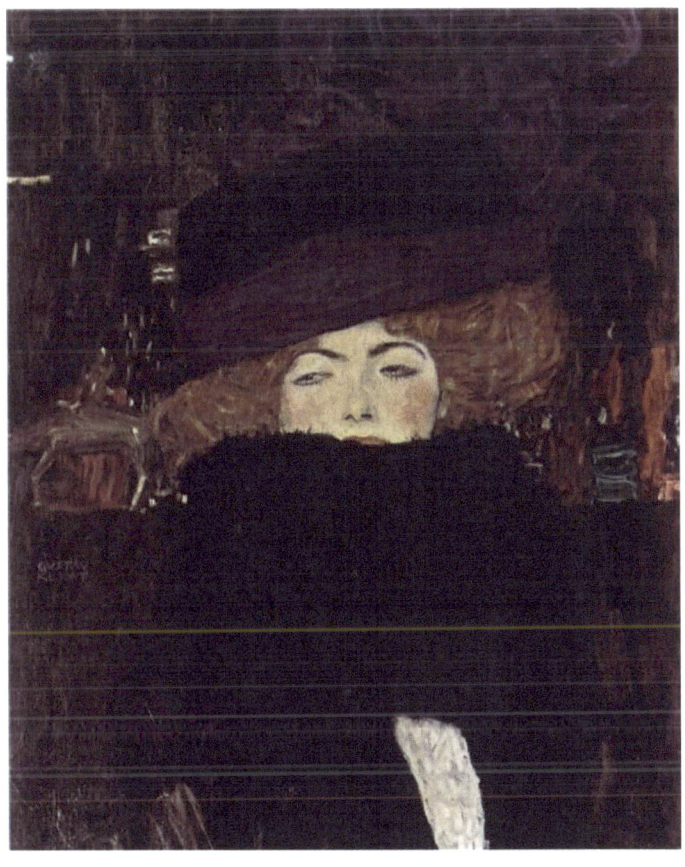

Lady with Hat and Featherboa
1909, oil on canvas

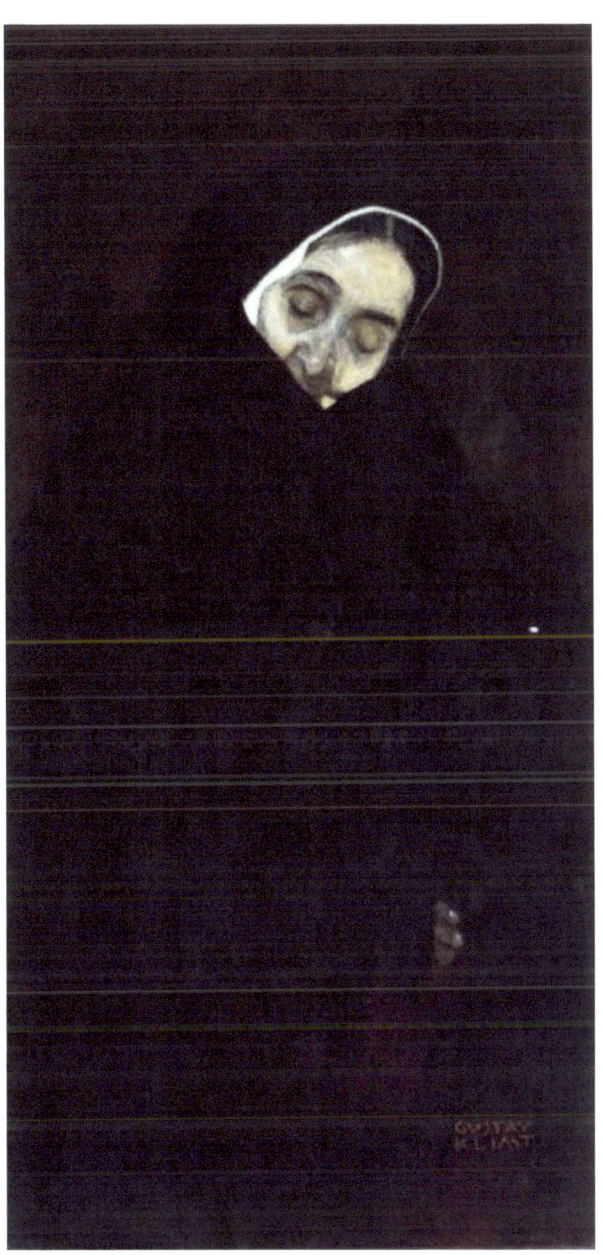

Old Woman
1909, oil on canvas

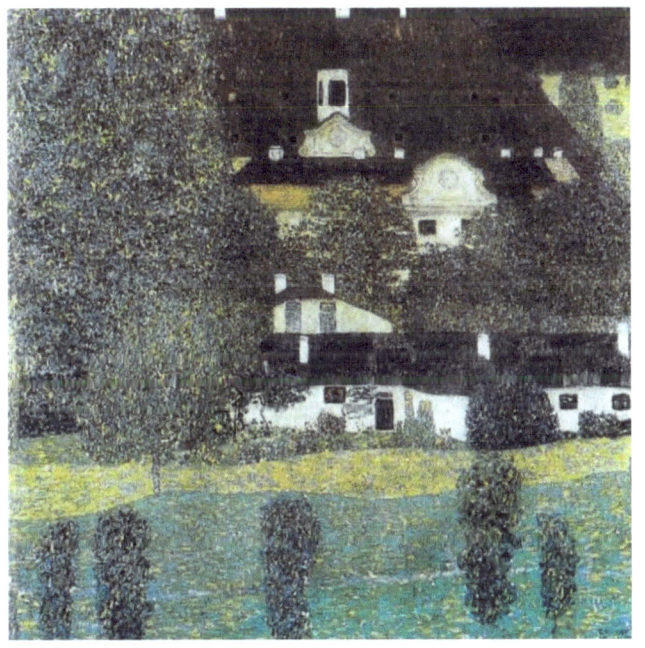

Castle Kammer on the Attersee, II
1909, oil on canvas

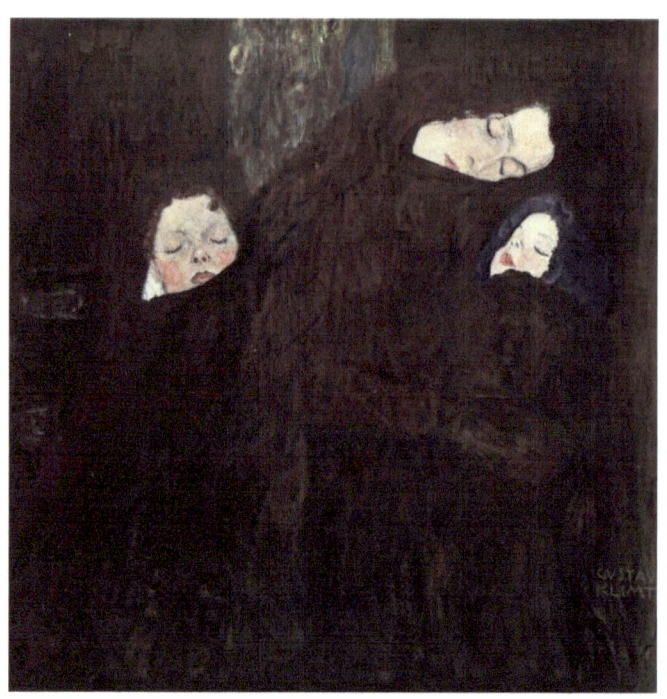

Mother with Children
1910, oil on canvas

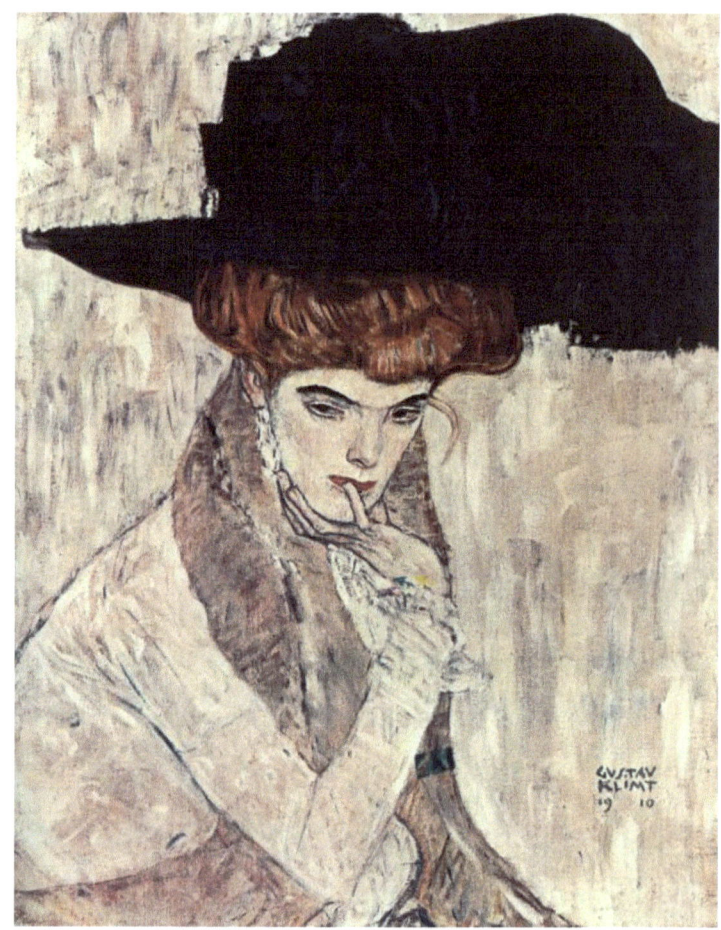

The Black Feather Hat
1910, oil on canvas

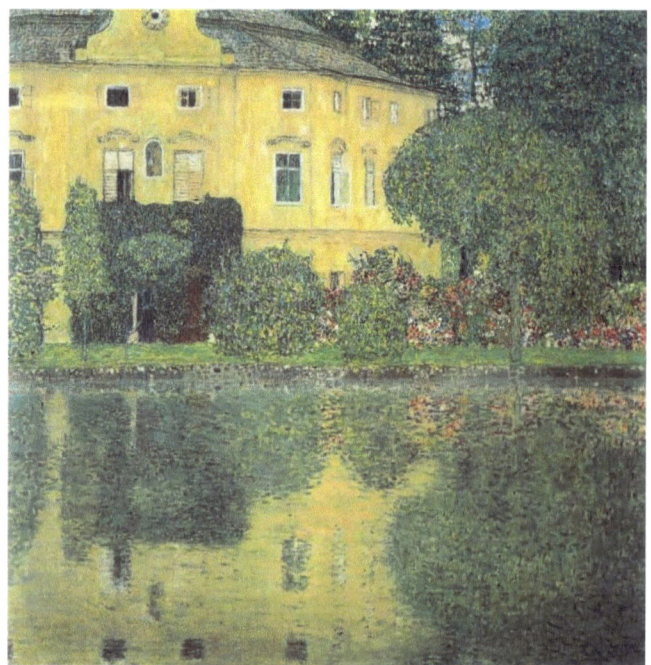

Schloss Kammer on the Attersee IV
1910, oil on canvas

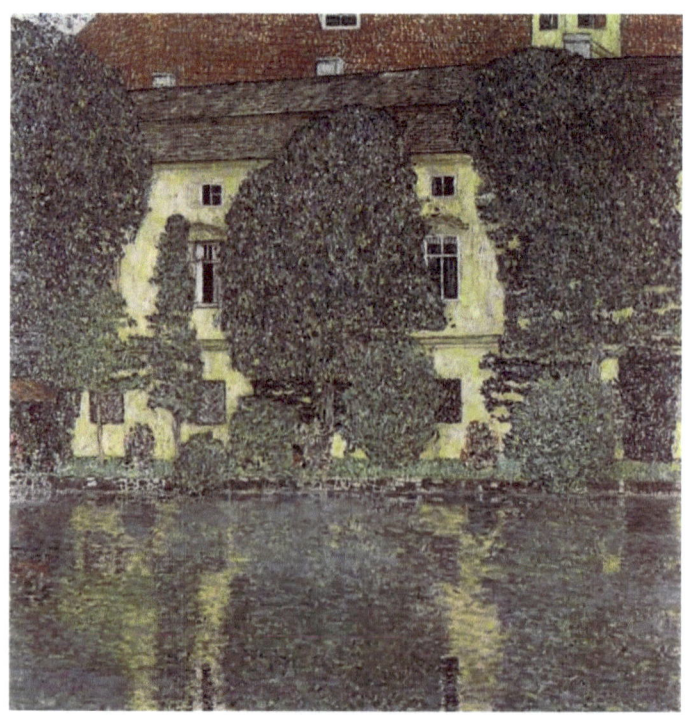

The Schloss Kammer on the Attersee, III
1910, oil on canvas

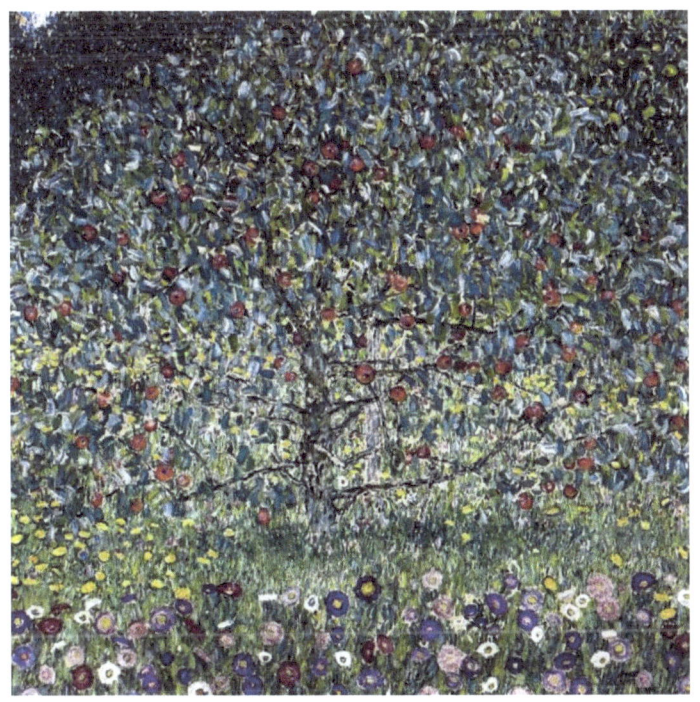

Apple Tree, I
1912, oil on canvas

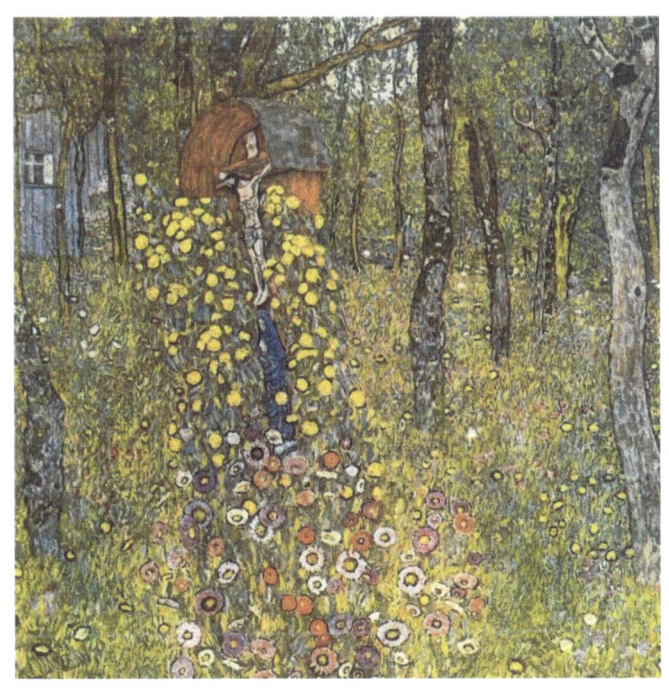

Farm Garden with Crucifix
1912, oil on canvas

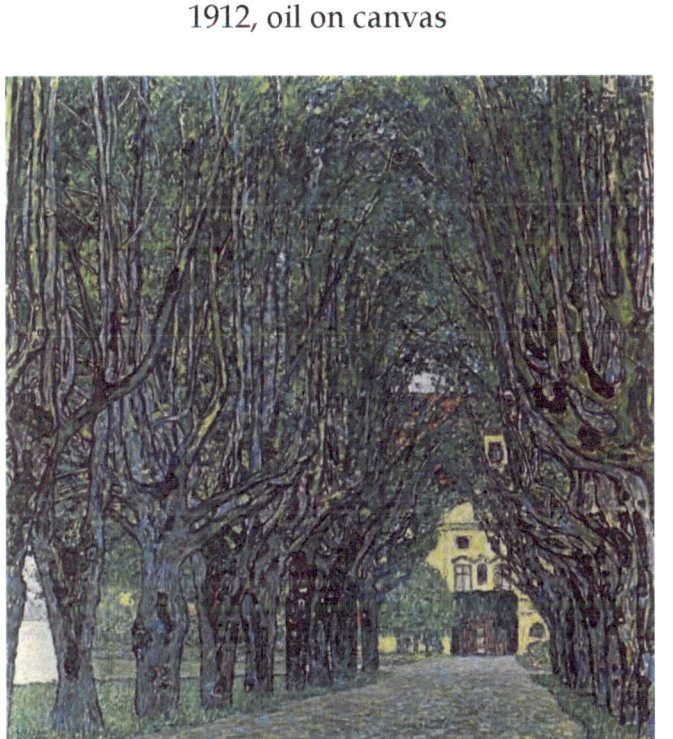

Avenue of Schloss Kammer Park
1912, oil on canvas

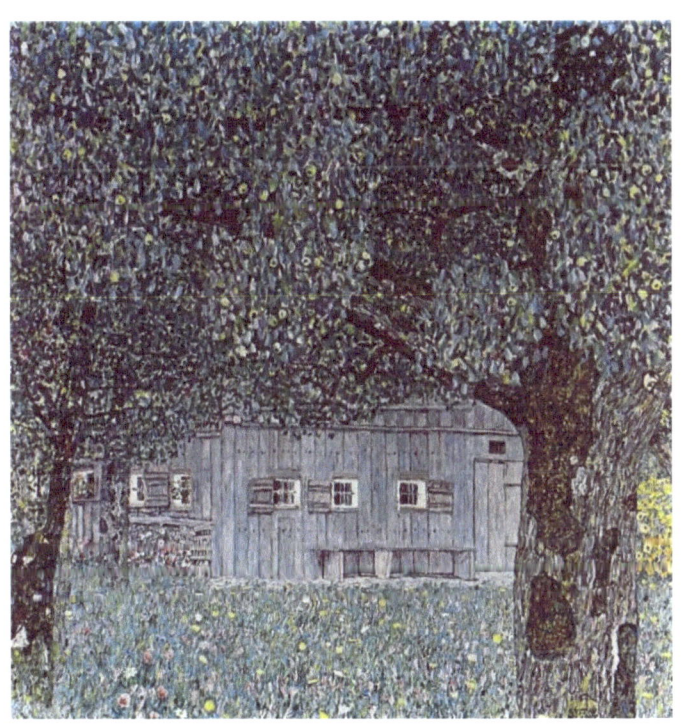

Farmhouse in Upper Austria
1912, oil on canvas

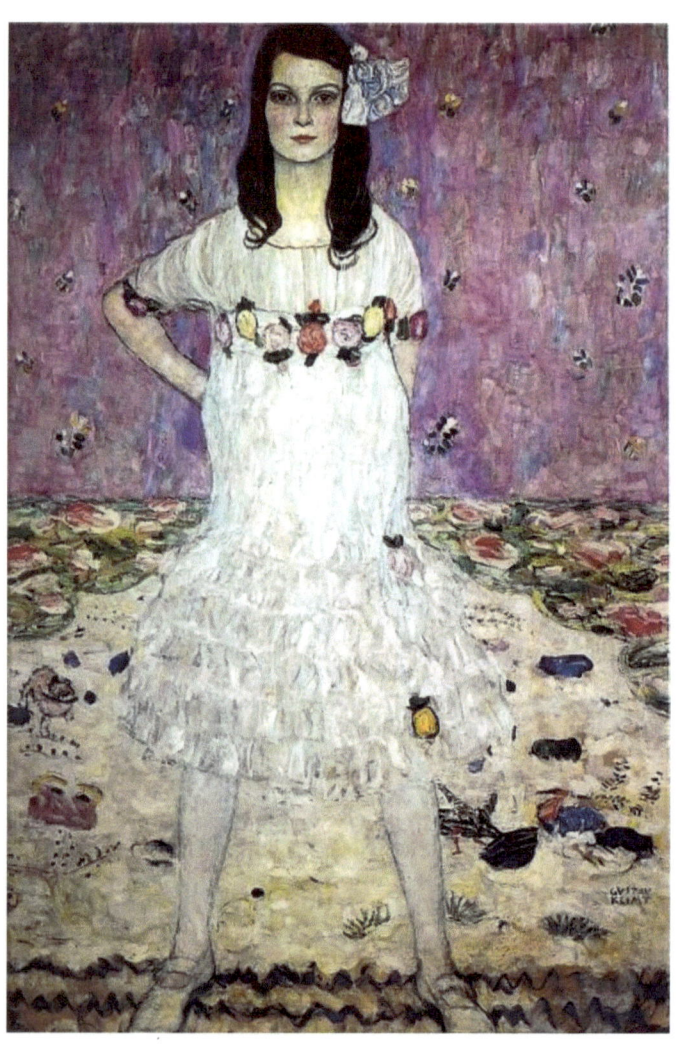

Mada Primavesi
1912, oil on canvas

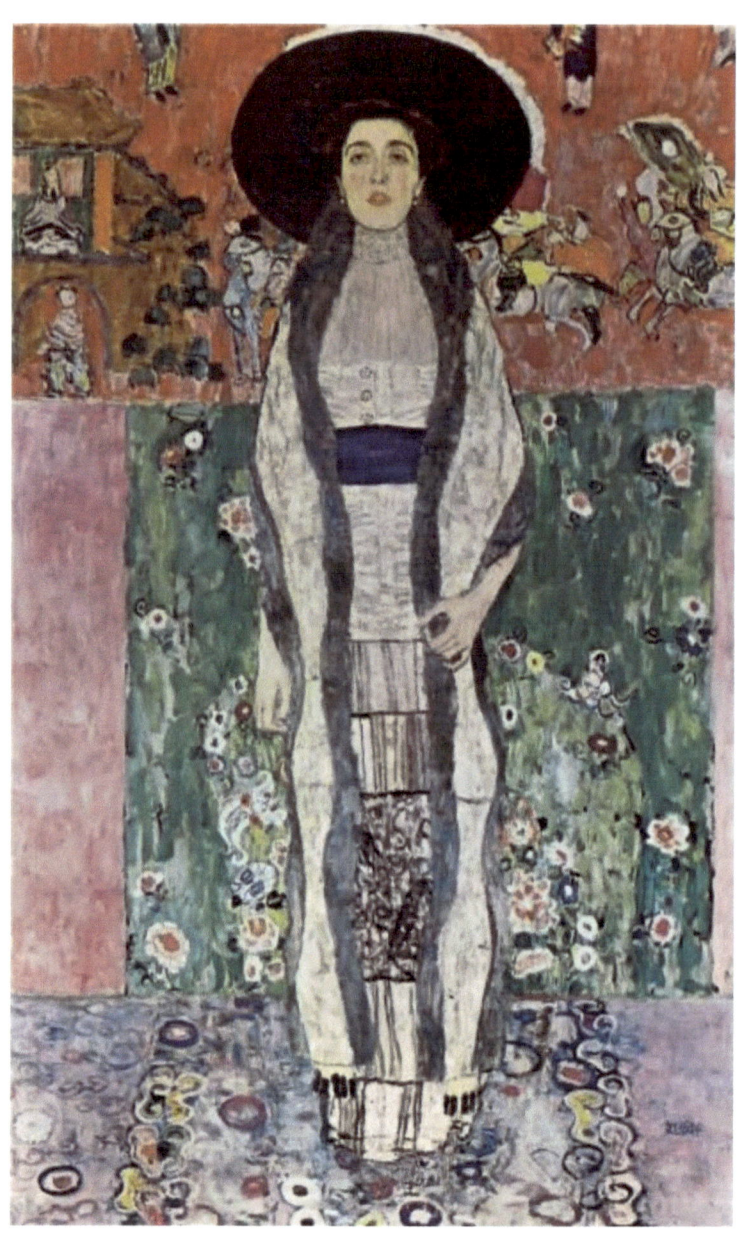

Portrait of Adele Bloch-Bauer II
1912, oil on canvas

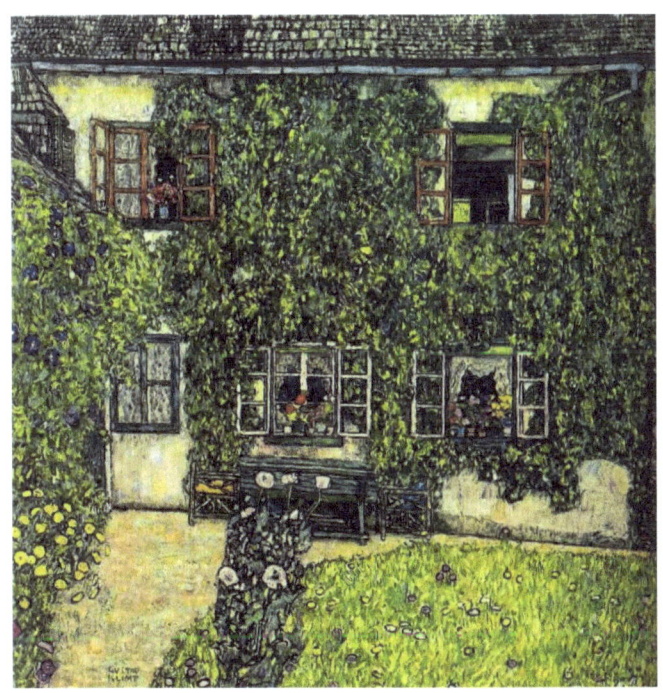

The House of Guardaboschi
1912, oil on canvas

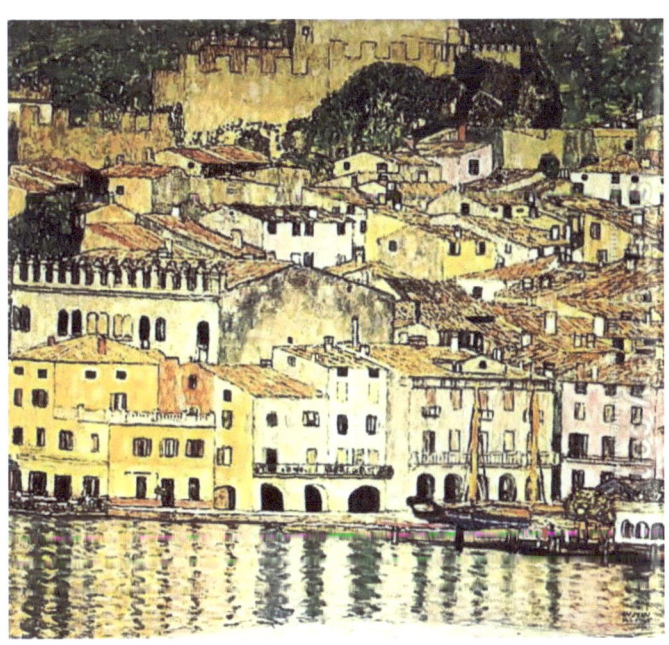

Malcesine on Lake Garda
1912, oil on canvas

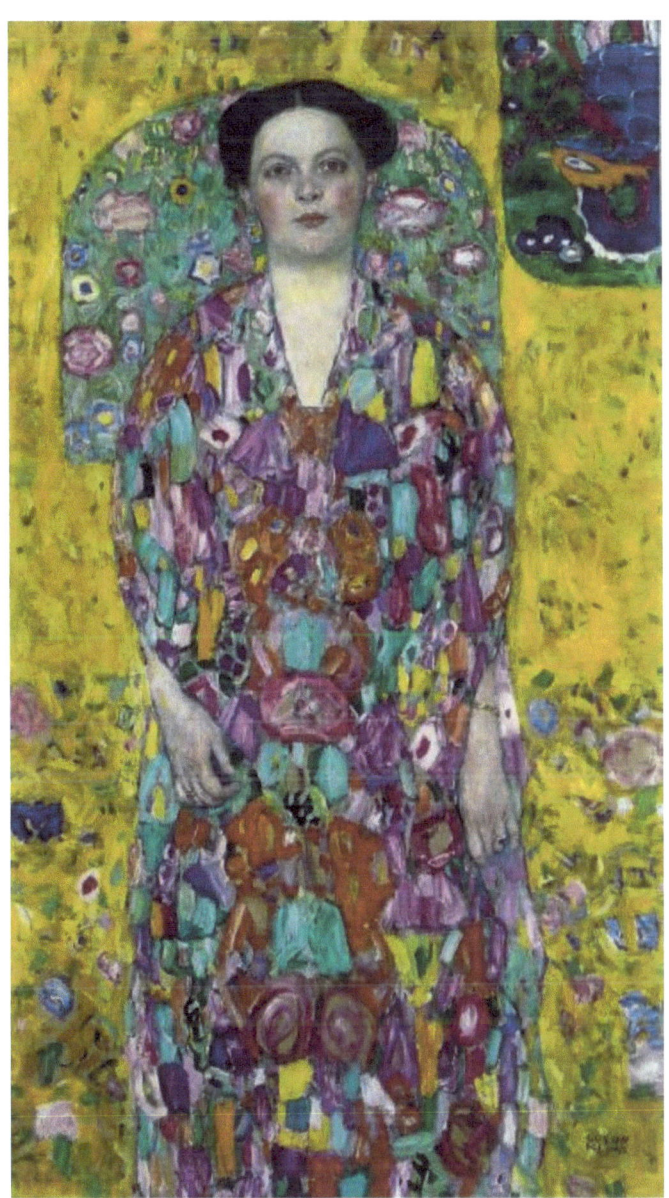

Portrait of Eugenia Primavesi
1913, oil on canvas

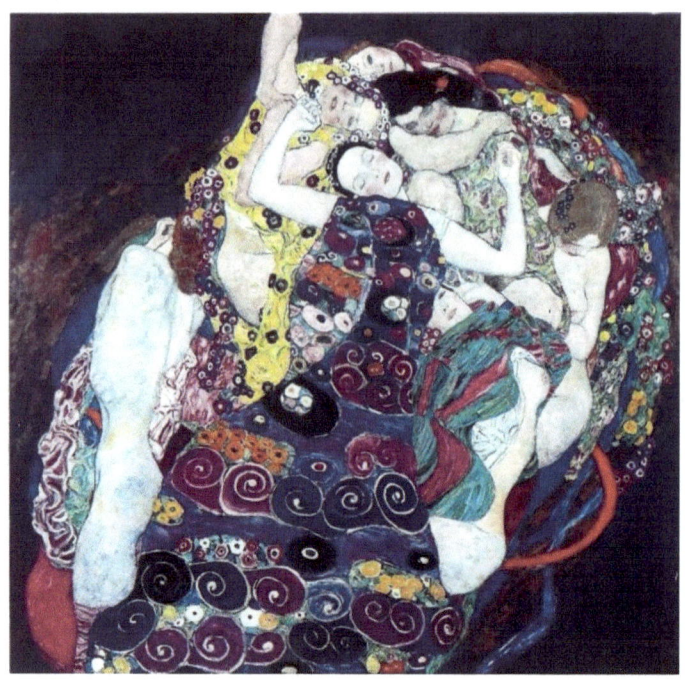

The Virgin
1913, oil on canvas

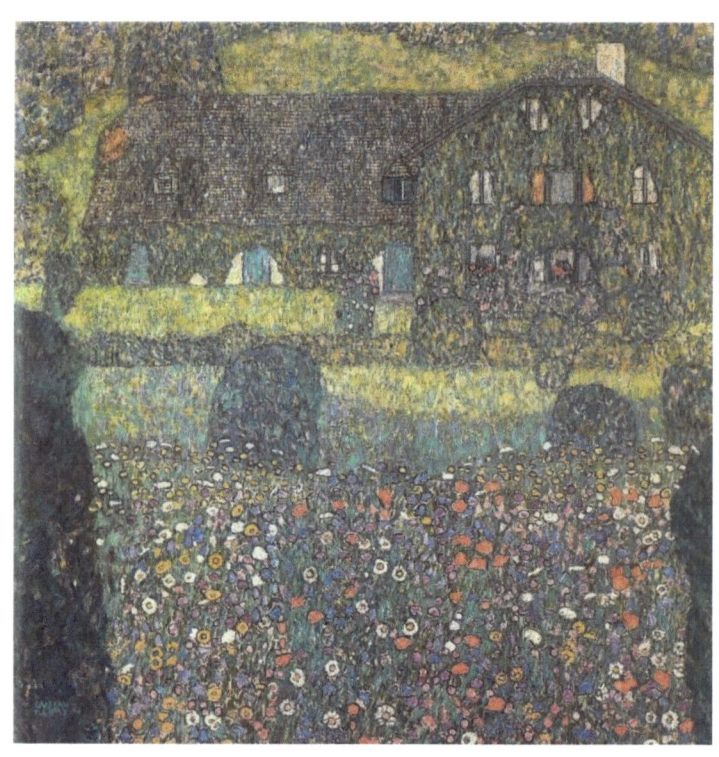

Country House by the Attersee
1914, oil on canvas

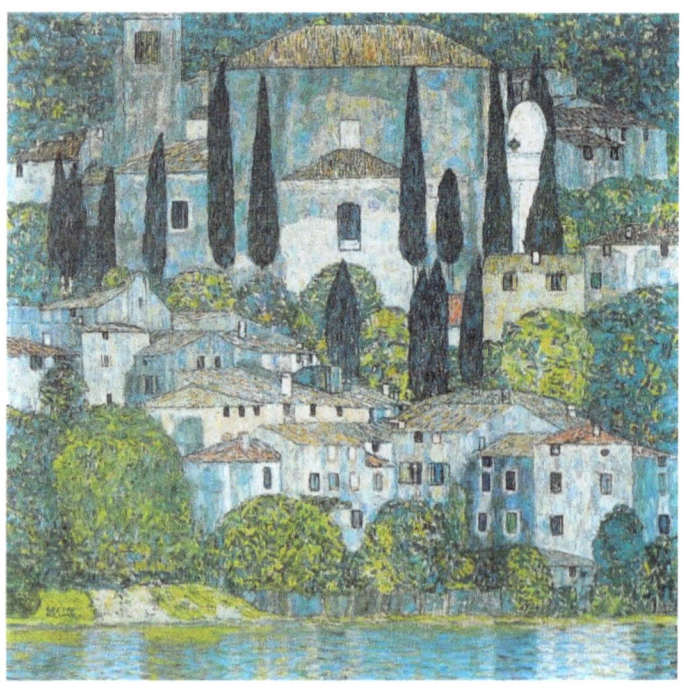

Chruch in Cassone
1913, oil on canvas

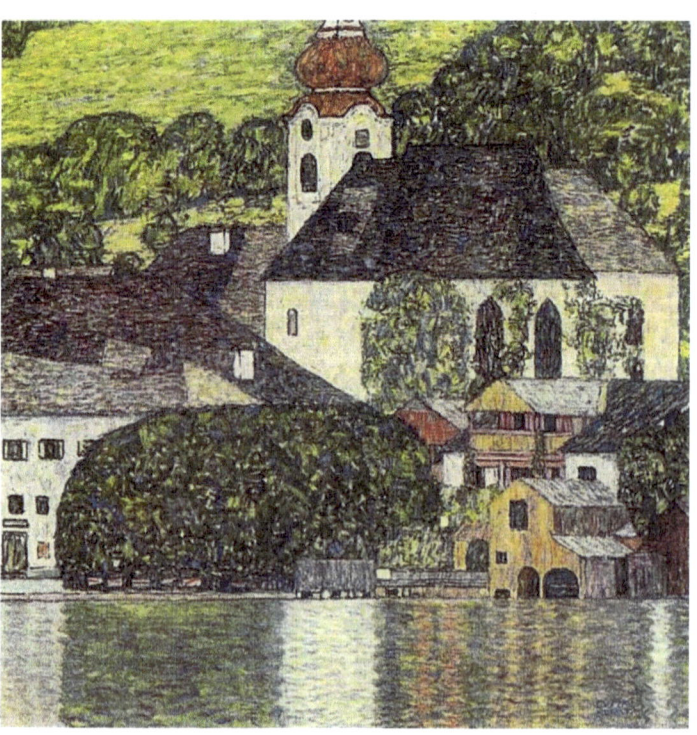

Church in Unterach on the Attersee
1916, oil on canvas

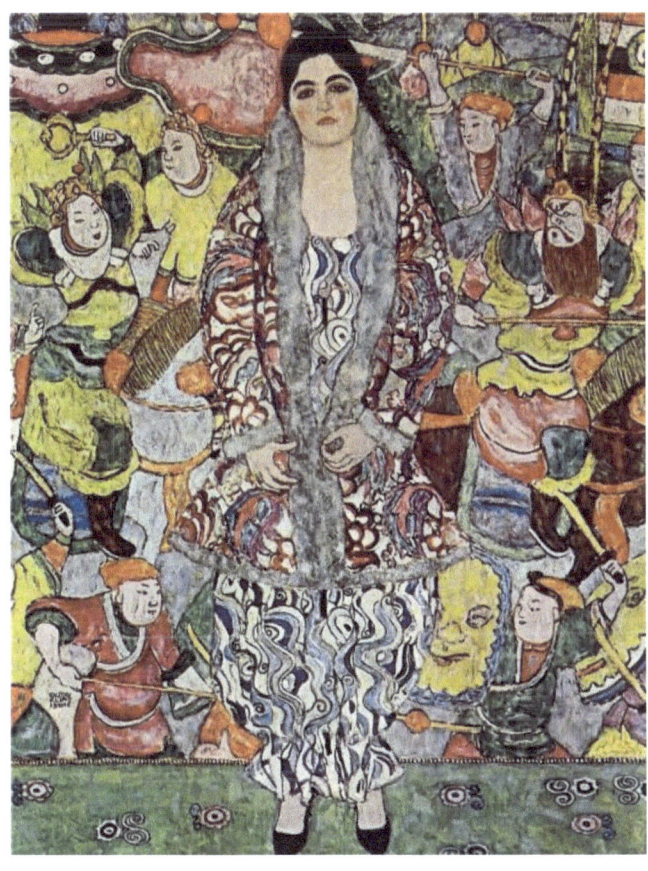

Fredericke Maria Beer
1916, oil on canvas

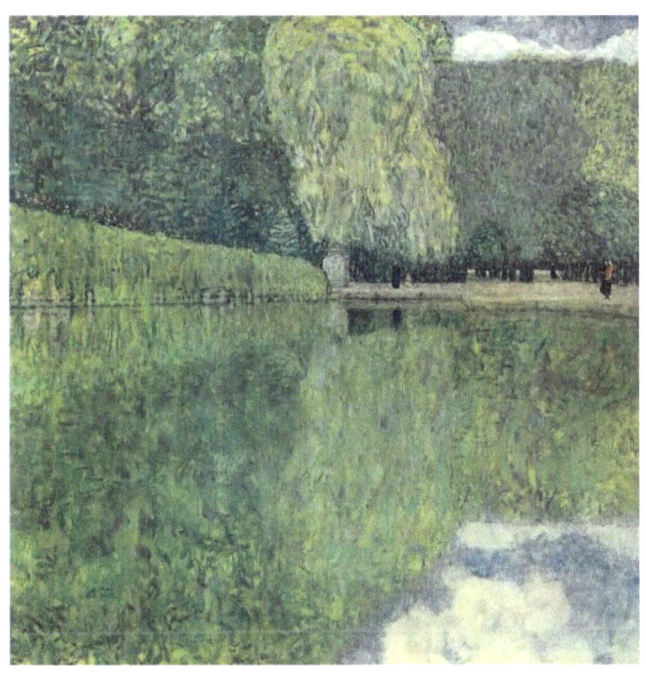

Park of Schönbrunn
1916, oil on canvas

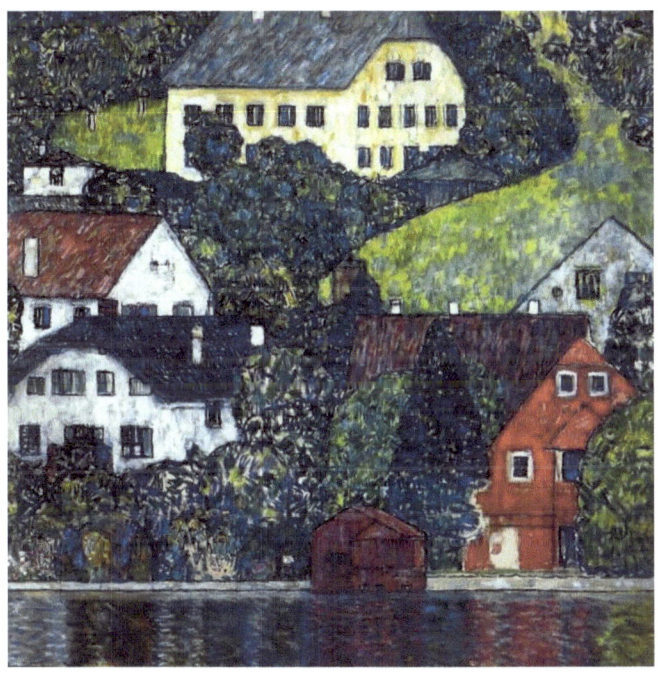

Houses at Unterach on the Attersee
1916, oil on canvas

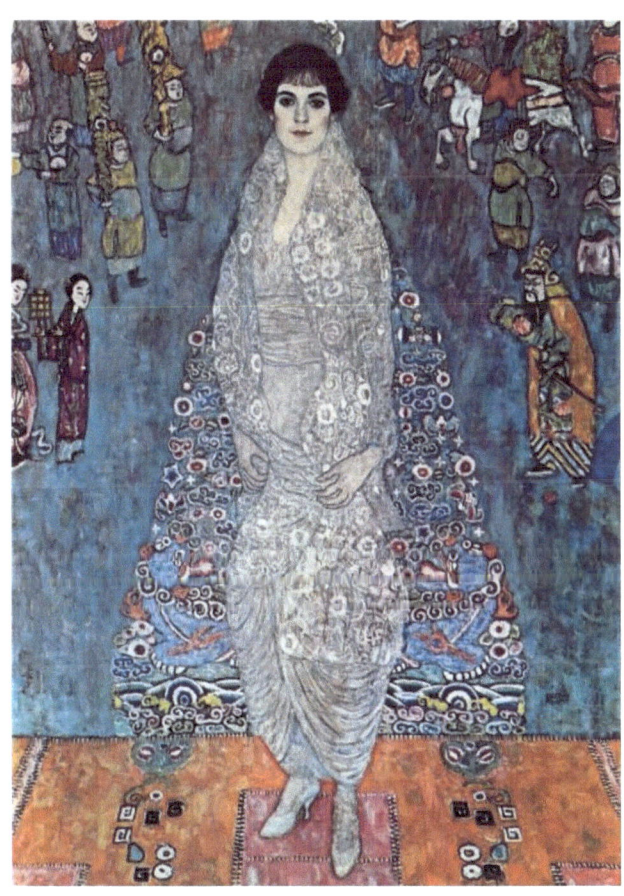

Portrait of Baroness Elisabeth Bachofen-Echt
1916, oil on canvas

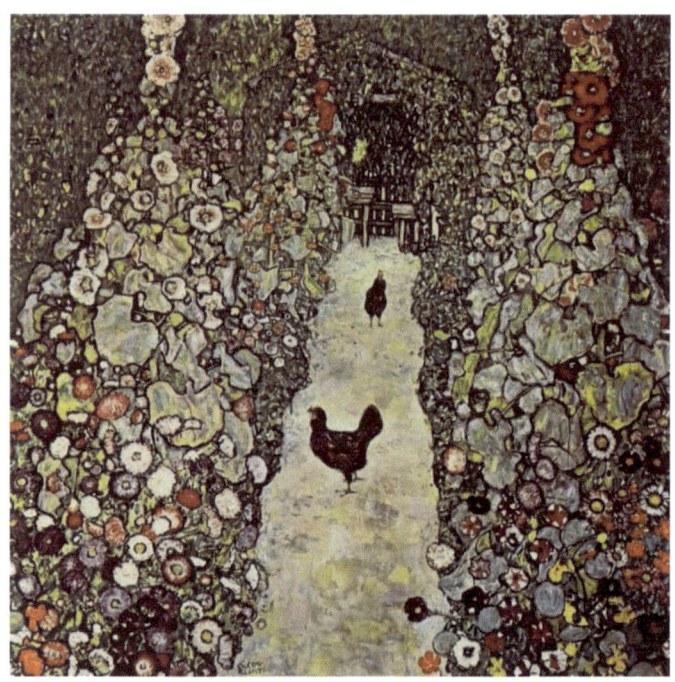

Garden with Roosters
1917, oil on canvas

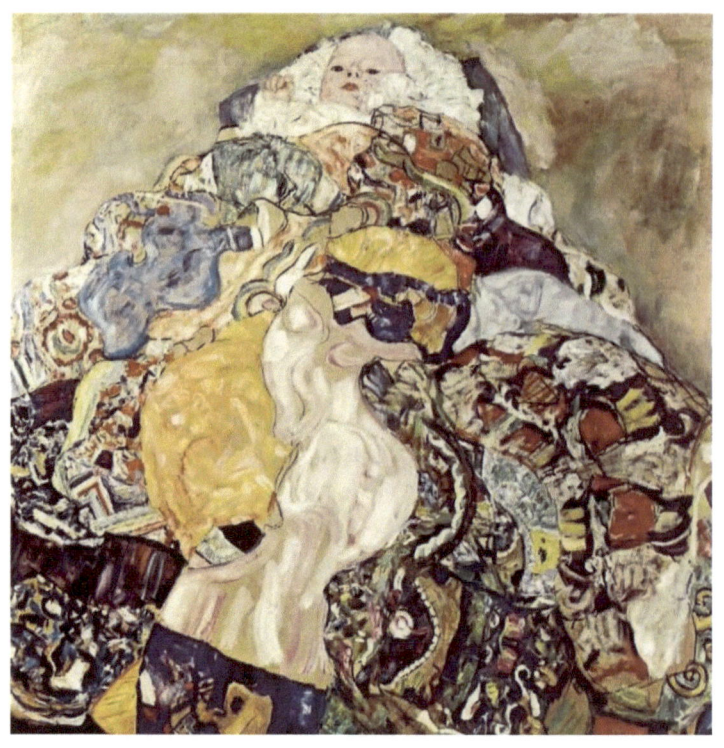

Baby
1918, oil on canvas

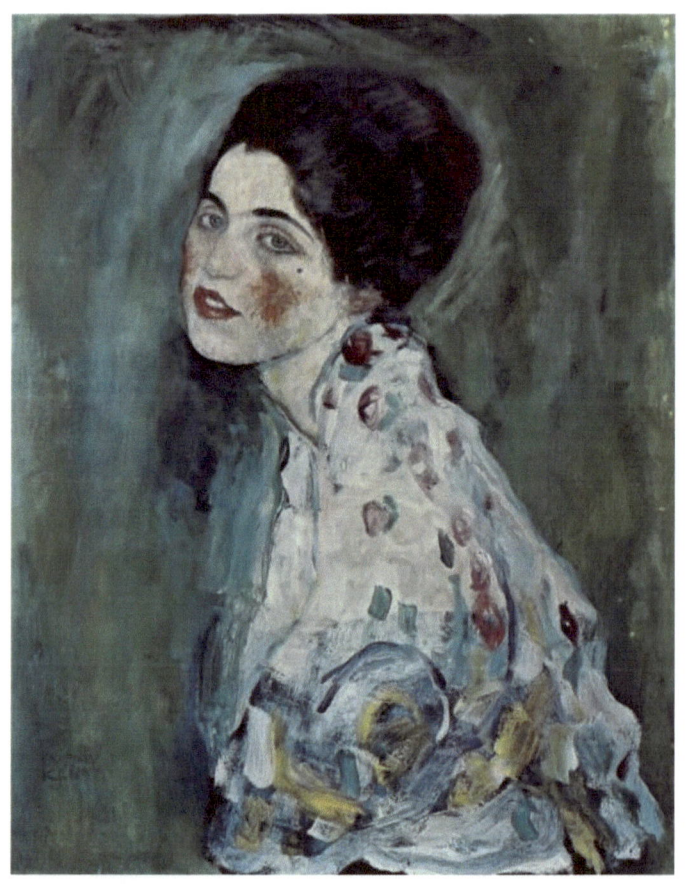

Portrait of a Lady
1917, oil on canvas

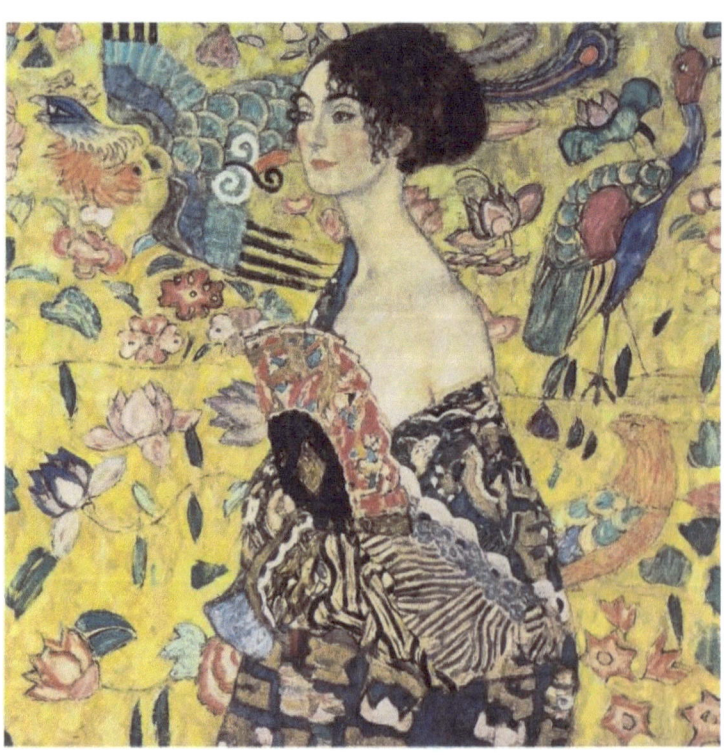

Lady with Fan
1918, oil on canvas

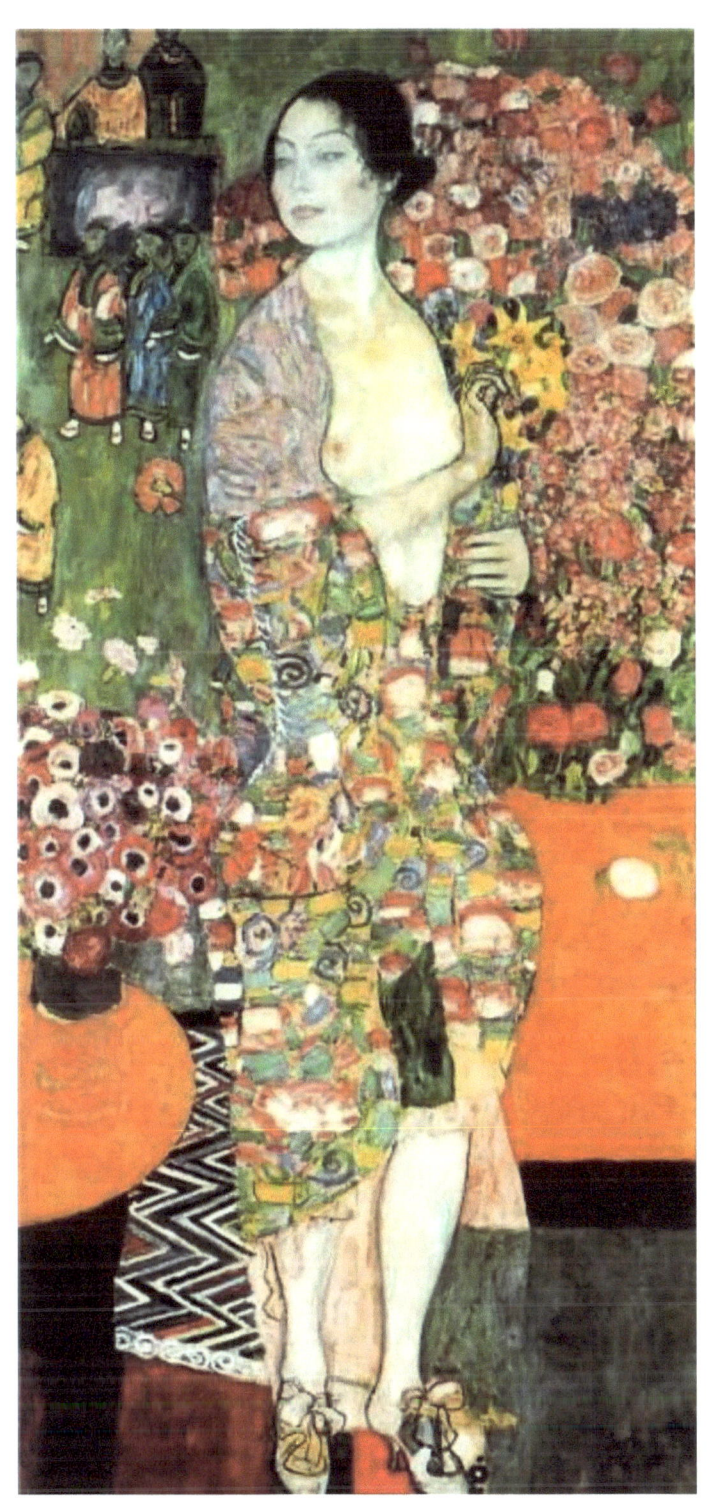

The dancer
1918, oil on canvas

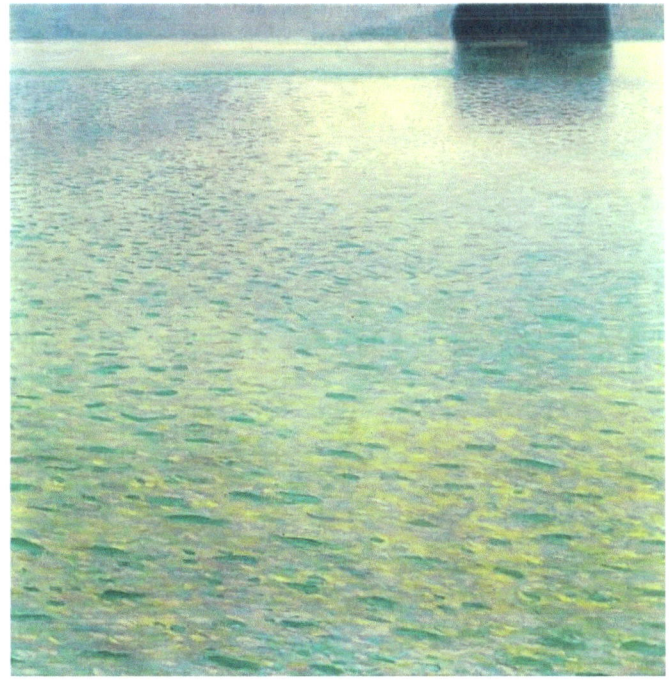

Island in the Attersee, N.d., oil on canvas

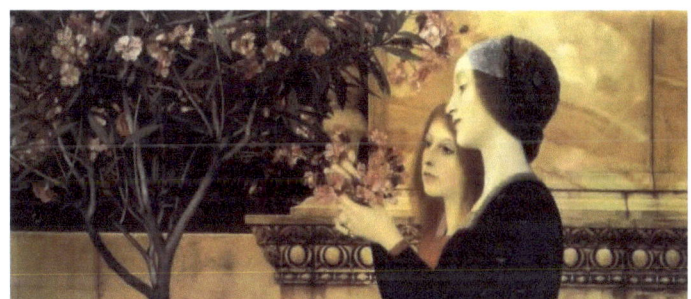

Two Girls with An Oleander, N.d., oil on
canvas